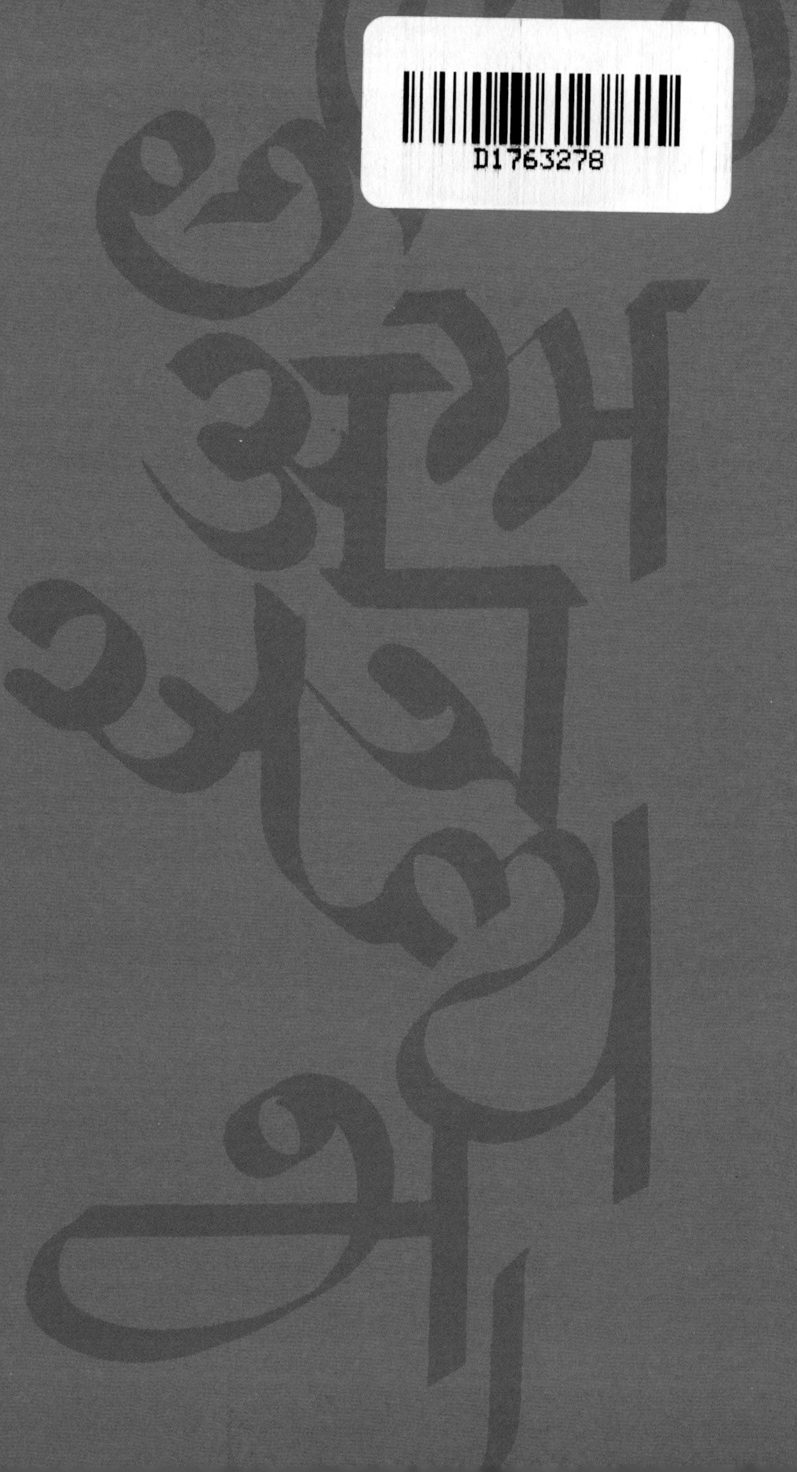

INDIA

Books by G. N. Devy

Mahabharata: The Epic and the Nation
The Crisis Within: Knowledge and Education in India
Critical Thought
After Amnesia
In Another Tongue
Of Many Heroes: An Indian Essay in Literary Historiography
Indian Literary Criticism: Theory and Interpretation
A Nomad Called Thief: Reflections in Adivasi Silence
The G. N. Devy Reader
Countering Violence
The Question of Silence

Edited by G. N. Devy

The Indians: Histories of a Civilization (with Tony Joseph and Ravi Korisettar)
India Between Tradition and Modernity (co-editor)
Painted Words: An Anthology of Tribal Literature (editor)
The People's Linguistic Survey of India (chief editor)

INDIA
A LINGUISTIC CIVILIZATION

G. N. DEVY

ALEPH

ALEPH

ALEPH BOOK COMPANY
An independent publishing firm
promoted by *Rupa Publications India*

First published in India in 2024
by Aleph Book Company
7/16 Ansari Road, Daryaganj
New Delhi 110 002

Copyright © G. N. Devy 2024

All rights reserved.

The author has asserted his moral rights.

The views and opinions expressed in this book are the
author's own and the facts are as reported by him,
which have been verified to the extent possible, and the
publishers are not in any way liable for the same.

The publisher has used its best endeavours to ensure that
URLs for external websites referred to in this book are
correct and active at the time of going to press. However,
the publisher has no responsibility for the websites and
can make no guarantee that a site will remain live or that
the content is or will remain appropriate.

No part of this publication may be reproduced,
transmitted, or stored in a retrieval system, in any form or
by any means, without permission in writing from Aleph
Book Company.

ISBN: 978-93-93852-67-0

1 3 5 7 9 10 8 6 4 2

Printed in India

This book is sold subject to the condition that it shall not,
by way of trade or otherwise, be lent, resold, hired out, or
otherwise circulated without the publisher's prior consent
in any form of binding or cover other than that in which it
is published.

CONTENTS

1. India as a Linguistic Civilization — 1
2. Language and the State — 57
3. Memory and Oral Traditions — 106
4. Digital Future, Translation, and Knowledge — 142

Notes — 181

Bibliography — 187

1

INDIA AS A LINGUISTIC CIVILIZATION

INDIA AS CULTURAL SPACE

There is a raging debate in the country about the 'idea of India', though the phrase is rarely explained by those who use it. Grasping its many meanings is left to the listener's imagination, the context in which it is used, and the audiences for whom it is used. At times, it refers to the Indian republic founded upon the Constitution. At other times, it evokes the grand vision of a timeless India, with all its diversities and all the hazy past epochs. It may refer to the many origins of India's diverse populations and cultures, or it may even be used as a synonym for what we think was or is the Indian 'civilization'. Thinking of a civilization is by no means easy; and certainly not after Sigmund Freud's century-old *Civilisation and its Discontents* (1929) placing 'civilization' as the antagonist of 'ego', placing individuals under a psychological imprisonment, and after Michel Foucault's *Madness and Civilization* (1961). In the context of India, the use of the term 'civilization' is even more problematic since the entire edifice of colonialism was built on the deceptive premise of the white man's burden of 'civilizing' India. However, setting aside these negative (though revealing) connotations of the term, if one were to strictly adhere to the dictionary definition, one finds that the term is rooted in the Latin *civitas*, what later became the English 'civil', pointing firmly to city as the basis of civilization. In India, the city or the urban social structures, which first came into existence during the Indus period, had reached its pinnacle during the six centuries—from the twenty-fourth to the nineteenth century BCE—and declined by the eighteenth century BCE. That was followed by a hiatus lasting half a millennium, a time about which we have scant knowledge. The next known phase of India's prehistory emerges with the *Rigveda*, around the fourteenth century BCE, when India had entered a new social system in which cities did emerge, but the larger population of India had chosen the village structures as its long-term civilizational choice. Since then, and until the era of colonialism—during which cities were once again given prominence—for over three millennia, most of the knowledge production, artistic expression, and metaphysical meditations continued to reside in remote and rural places rather than in the cities that came into existence at various times during this long period of Indian history. Seen from this limited perspective of binding civilization to urbanism, the term 'civilization' is not adequate to encompass India's past. However, by 'civilization' if one implies 'all that was there, great and not so great'—a pervasive and binding cultural thread—one has to invoke, in India's case, language plurality as being that thread: the élan vital, the core, substance, and essence of the idea of India. At the same time, the history of language in India as an instrument of domination, resulting in severe social exclusion of masses, points to the 'civilizing' role that language played in the sense in which Freud and Foucault use the term.

It should be unnecessary to add that the 'idea of India' cannot ever be conceptualized as a singular. Plurality and diversity are its inalienable attributes. Similarly, it is futile to seek for some imagined and idealized 'pure origins'. Cultural diversity in India can hardly be interpreted or internalized by placing it under scrutiny, guided by the question of ontological chronologies. Any history of India stands to suffer loss if it gets nailed to chronological excesses. The issue of origins is to be understood not only from the perspective of time but also from the perspective of space. Interpretations of India's past and present get parodied when one brings in the binaries such as 'inside–outside' and 'self and other'. The 'idea of India' can be rendered lifeless if one were to attempt opening it up in terms of the native Indians and the others who came here from elsewhere. The presence that India has been cannot be adequately understood by conceptualizing it as a measurable ethnographic and cultural territory. It is much better grasped if it is viewed like the vast oceans between fixed territories, or as the vast space between different planets. Of course, these are mere metaphors and not to be taken in their literal sense. In any case, human populations have migrated across continents since the time the *Homo sapiens* emerged as a biological species in remote prehistoric times. Considering that the phenomenon of populations mix dominated the prehistoric, proto-historic and historic epochs of human past, it is nearly impossible to settle the question of the 'original' population in any place on the face of the earth. The area we presently call India is no exception. Besides, the geographical expanse that we call today as India has not necessarily been exactly identical with the areas that were described in various phases of proto-history and history as 'Ind' or 'India'. It is necessary, therefore, to be mindful that the 'idea of India' cannot but be a plural noun, with the range of plurality increasing as one tends to comprehend India over increasingly larger durations of time. However, there is a certain advantage in casting the 'idea of India' over an extended period, for such a perspective facilitates a clearer understanding of its long and seemingly continuous trajectory.

A gestalt view of the epistemic shifts in India's self-perception can unravel what has been and continues to be India. The epistemic shifts can be described in various ways, such as analysing the material culture, interpreting philosophical productions, narrating political histories or tabulating demographic variations. One of these approaches would be, to examine what India was doing with its languages, and how various languages impacted India's epistemic architecture in different epochs in the past. It can be divided into four broadly demarcated language periods, in turn, forming the basis of India's epistemic foundations:

1. The long and hazy period, from the time *Homo sapiens* started inhabiting the subcontinent, till the decline of the first civilization, a period giving rise to exclusively 'oral' and 'natural' languages.
2. The period of language mix beginning around 1500 BCE

and developing into 'written' and 'literary' languages, running up to the end of the first millennium.
3. The period of the rise of the languages at present described as 'modern Indian languages', roughly beginning around 1000 CE and ending around 1800 CE.
4. The period that witnessed the making of India as a union of linguistic states dominated by print technology.

THE INDIA OF NATURAL LANGUAGES

Since the nineteenth century till the early twentieth century, history and archaeology had remained fairly separate scholarly pursuits. Archaeology was considered to be the science of reconstructing the past through tangible evidence such as rocks, bricks, buildings, beads, skeletons, metallic objects, and seeds. It was focused on the descriptive study of specific locations, and its aim was to arrive at how people lived in the past eras, which had eluded the grasp of history. History, on the other hand, acknowledged that literary and linguistic evidence came down to us in oral traditions, manuscripts, coins, and inscriptions. Archaeology was predominantly non-linguistic and history was predominantly lingual. The significant disparity in study methods between the two branches of historical inquiry led people to commonly perceive the past, which was examined by archaeology, as prehistory. That situation has changed over the last few decades, after human genetics notably heightened awareness regarding the movements of humanity's earliest ancestors. In particular, we now know a lot more about the spread of *Homo sapiens* and the growth in their populations in different parts of the world since the Holocene some twelve millennia ago. Tony Joseph's *Early Indians: The Story of Our Ancestors and Where We Came From* (2018) synthesizes all the recent research in human genetics and demonstrates the movements of the 'Out of Africa' humans who made several continents their homes. He comments on four major migrations into India during the last 70,000 years. The first of these was the pre-Holocene migration all the way from Africa. The next took place in the millennia following the commencement of Holocene and within Asia. He cites Peter Bellwood (2013) who observes, 'The second class of major prehistoric migrations happened much later, after the glacial period ended around 12,000 years ago, when some modern human population took to agriculture in different parts of the world.' Not every group took to agriculture at the same time, and not all agriculture was equally productive or beneficial. For example, those who were in situations that enabled them to take up cereal cultivation in Mesopotamia, Egypt, India, and China were in a more advantageous position than, say, those who took to cultivating tubers, yams, and bananas, as in the Pacific Islands or Southeast Asia. And wherever modern humans took to cereal cultivation, what followed was a population explosion. After people settled down to farming and found ways to increase productivity, human fertility and numbers increased dramatically, leading to migrations. 'This set of farming-related migrations or Neolithic migrations as they are called, left strong marks on human demography everywhere.' (Devy et al., 2023).

The spread of agriculture to India, and later within India, according to plant archaeologist Satish Naik, can be dated back to 9,000 to 8,000 years ago (Devy et al., 2023). Human settlements, along with domestication of cattle, around cultivated areas, would have formed the foundation of the villages in India. Arati Deshpande-Mukherjee reports, 'In South Asia, Neolithic culture is identified as early as the seventh millennium BCE, at Mehrgarh in Pakistan. Here the beginning of settled life—agriculture, use of ceramics and domesticated animals—has been documented. In its early levels, during the ceramic phase, exploitation of animals is recorded, but in the succeeding phase, ceramics and the presence of domestic cattle, sheep, and goat is seen.' (Devy et al., 2023). She adds, 'It is established that domestic cattle were used in northwest South Asia by the seventh millennium BCE following which, by the third millennium BCE, cattle pastoralism was quite common in the Indus valley and adjoining areas.' (Ibid). What is interesting to note here is that the agrarian communities which spread over India prior to the second millennium BCE had their languages—*Homo sapiens* have been using complex languages for the past 70,000 years. In fact, the ability for the acquisition of language was one of the factors that made the prehistoric migrations possible at all. Therefore, to assume the origins of the early agrarian communities in India from the ninth to the third millennia BCE should need no specific corroboration.

Though we have neither any written nor oral evidence as to the characteristics of the languages used by the pre-Sanskrit groups in India, it won't be illogical to assume that they created a profusion of nature- and agriculture-related terminologies. Given the nature of the entire migration, slow spread of agriculture and habitation formation in the extended geographic region of South Asia, the existence of hundreds of languages cannot be ruled out. Thus, diversity as a cultural value, a symbiotic relation with cattle and other domesticated animals, the respectful attitude to plants and closely formed clans, and the subsequent Sanskrit term *gotra* literally meaning 'cattle related family identity', formed a prehistoric India, with diversity of natural languages being one of its overarching attributes. We do not have adequate technological tools to access the pre-Indus languages. The languages spoken by the Indus Valley residents themselves have remained an unresolved mystery. If and when it becomes possible in the future to place all the existing mother tongues in India together and to scientifically reconstruct their historical, phonetic and syntactic evolution, we may get access to at least some of those pre-Indus and pre-Vedic languages. As of now, no Indian language research establishment is equipped to carry out such a mammoth investigation. One would think that the emergence of what the nineteenth-century archaeologists have termed 'civilization'—the Indus Valley urban habitats and those who populated them—became the force to bring about a radical shift in the world-view of the people in India during the third millennium BCE. That fundamental shift had to wait till the arrival of the Sanskrit language in India. The mutual entanglement of Sanskrit and the language varieties that were spoken in India during the second half of the second and the first millennium BCE resulted in that shift.

THE LANGUAGE MIX IN ANCIENT INDIA

The long period from the fifteenth century BCE to the third century BCE once again created an idea of India, significantly different from the one that had previously taken shape over tens of millennia. This period saw a new tradition of oral memory, ideas of divinity, a new social stratification, and a new arrangement of power. Many material factors were responsible for the new formation of India in that era, generally designated by historians as 'Ancient India'. The use of metals, first bronze and later iron, among those material factors, is considered the most crucial by archaeologists in the shaping of ancient India. The use of metals played a similar role in ushering the prehistoric populations in different continents into its history. They certainly impacted lifestyles of people and provided the ground for the emergence of kingship and the state. Yet, the social stratification in India in terms of *varna* and *jati* during the period does not have many exact matches in most other geographical areas of the old world. The rise of the *varnas* and the *jatis* can be better explained by looking at the long, drawn-out, and utterly complex process of the language mix, which characterizes the two-and-a-half-millennia period of India's ancient history.

The question as to when exactly the Dravidian and Indo-Aryan came in contact may be an unresolved matter;

but it is beyond doubt that a proto-Dravidian language variety had been in existence in South India, and quite likely in various other parts of India as well, prior to its coming in contact with Sanskrit. This language had several features which were quite distinct from the linguistic features of the Sanskrit of the Indo-Aryan language family. As summarized by the scholar of Dravidian Linguistics, K. Rangan, 'The pronouns, numerals, the conjugation of verbs with tense and person, gender agreement suffixes, the conjugation of nouns with case suffixes, the arrangement of words in sentences are basic and they differ from the structure of Sanskrit and other Indo-Aryan languages.' Besides, he explains: 'The negative occurs pre-verbally in Indo-Aryan languages but in Dravidian languages, it is post-verbal. The verbs in Dravidian languages are conjugated for negative voice. The absence of relative pronouns in the construction of relative clauses is a marked difference between Indo-Aryan and Dravidian languages.' (Devy et al., 2023)

There are several other important differences between the two. The point is that the two, Sanskrit and the early-ancient Dravidian developed closer associations with other languages over time. In addition to the Dravidian language(s), there also existed in India during the second millennium BCE languages of the Austro-Asiatic people who had migrated to South Asia after the 'Last Glacial Maximum', around the eighteenth millennium BCE. They came into India in two distinct waves of migration (Devy et al., 2023). Till the middle of the second millennium BCE, these languages had stayed apart, with little interaction among them. The arrival of the speakers of Indo-Aryan in several waves during the second millennium BCE, after the decline of the Indus Civilization, increased the interaction and generated a new era that can be described as the Age of Language-Mix. In addressing the question of the origin of Indo-Aryan, Meera Visvanathan points out that increased mobility and new military technology enabled the spread of the language across a vast geographical area, a phenomenon unprecedented in any of the earlier millennia.

> While much of the scholarly ink has been spilt on the question of the Indo-European homeland, the archaeological and linguistic evidence taken together points to the origin of Proto-Indo-European on the Pontiac Caspian Steppes around 4000 BCE.... The reconstructed vocabulary of Proto-Indo-European shows a culture of pastoralists, in which horses and wheeled vehicles played an important role. The spread of the Indo-European languages can thus be linked to the emergence of a highly mobile pastoralist culture in the Steppe region, even as points of divergence between the different branches of Indo-European are still improperly understood. Consequently, while claims still abound of Sanskrit being the ancestor of all Indo-European languages or the Indo-Aryans being indigenous to the Indian subcontinent, these cannot be accepted as they contravene the evidence (Devy et al., 2023).

The technology of rapid movement which the speakers of Indo-Aryan brought with them entailed not just a greater penetration into the Indian subcontinent, it also meant an increased ability to recall the spaces the migrants had previously inhabited. The spatial awareness of the speakers of the Indo-Aryan was essentially different from that of the speakers of the other languages in existence in India; it continued to remain different from the spatial awareness of the preceding waves of the indigenous peoples and the migrants to South Asia, the Iranian agrarians, the Austro-Asiatic communities, and the speakers of the Dravidian inhabitants in the South. This difference can be shown by citing side by side the numerous texts produced in Sanskrit and its contemporary texts produced in one of the non-Sanskrit languages. For instance, the *Brihadarnyaka* Upanishad of the sixth or seventh century BCE states: 'When one tears out the tree from its roots, the tree can grow no more' (verse 3:9). In essence, both the roots and the trunk hold equal significance in defining the character of a tree. As against this the *Samyutta Nikaya* (verse 15:1–2) reports that the Buddha (who belonged to the same period as the composition of the *Brihadarnyaka* Upanishad) had stated: 'There is no first beginning, no first beginning is knowable.' The question of 'the first cause' came to be of epistemic significance in the philosophies that emerged out of the language-mix during the first millennium BCE. The great importance attached to the abstract notion of '*para*', the outermost and the transcendent, in the metaphysics woven through the Upanishads and the epics composed in Sanskrit during that millennium, along with philosophies and thought-streams that denied the idea of transcendence in different parts of India, form the very heart of the country constructed during the age of the language-mix.

One way of grasping the precise nature of the language-mix is comparative literary study; the other is the study of pottery, particularly the one attached to sacred rituals. Considering that the dates for the ancient texts have remained in many cases not precisely determined, while the patterns and geographical locations of pottery are known with a greater certainty, an examination of the geographical locations of the exchange and the mutual influence and transition of pottery traditions in the subcontinent may provide a reliable idea of the language-mix and cultural encounters during the first-millennium India. This is so because the pottery types used by the Indo-Aryans, the Painted Grey Ware (PGW), differed from the Black and Red Ware (BRW) used by the prehistoric speakers in East and South India. In an admirably comprehensive study of ancient pottery, R. Balakrishnan comments:

> A map of the distribution of Black and Red Ware (BRW)...shall paint a broad picture of the spread and the direction of movements. The BRW of Gujarat takes an eastward turn and goes along the Narmada and reaches up until the eastern Gangetic plains. BRW spreads its presence very clearly in eastern India including Odisha, West Bengal and Assam. If we look at the map at this stage, we will find that areas under PGW resemble islands amidst the BRW spread in the three directions—southwest, south and east. When we plot the sites of BRW irrespective of the fact whether

it is associated with Megalithic or not, the pottery map of India gives a different picture. The island of PGW is far more apparent now as PGW had no presence in the south. However, the emergence of Northern Black Painted Ware (NBPW) coincides with the interaction of what can be called the erstwhile PGW or the Vedic Aryan culture with other indigenous BRW pottery cultures in Eastern India and its subsequent spread to other parts of the country. ...The complete absence of PGW in the Deep South and the presence of NBPW in Korkai, a Sangam Age archaeological site not far from Adichanallur, also offers clues to the distribution and chronology of NBPW in the South and by implication a time frame for the spread of later North Indian ideas to the Deep South, particularly Tamil Nadu (Balakrishnan, 2022).

The clash and collaboration between the ideas of space that the earliest form of Sanskrit had brought with it, and those that had emerged in the agrarian as well as the nomadic communities existing in India prior to the first millennium BCE, resulted in the divergence in their respective world views. The world-view that was prioritized in Sanskrit focused on the verticality of everything: the human body, the social order, the world of other animal and plant species, and the cosmos. The highest in the order was ascribed an imagined purity; the lowest, in contrast, impurity or pollution.

LANGUAGE AND SOCIAL SEGMENTATION
Linguistics alone does not suffice to fully elucidate why

the emergence of *varna* and caste as social markers got entrenched only in India, with the arrival of the Indo-Aryan language(s) in the subcontinent, and why these or such ideas did not emerge in other continents and geographical areas where the various branches of the Indo-Europeans had reached and settled. However, a sociolinguistic view of the Indian past during the first millennium points to the nature of the language-mix as an important cause for the vertical social segregation. The *Purusha Sukta* of the *Rigveda* is often cited as a clear statement forming the basis on which ancient social segregation was attempted. It describes the Purusha, the universe (of whom are born the *rig* and the *saman*—the Vedas), and later the horses, goats, sheep, and the other animals. Then, the gods divided Purusha—'from the mouth of the divided Purusha came the Brahmin; from the arms came the Rajanya; from the thighs came the Vaishya; and from the feet came the Shudra.'

Such genesis myths mark early literature, particularly the literature that comes to be seen as scriptural, in every civilization. In the oral literature of tribal communities in India, we come across a variety of such creation myths and stories of the rise of the human species, implying a certain moral responsibility to keep the universe going. Every religion is based on its unique genesis story, and every culture or nation finds it nourishing to have its own version of how or where it began in some mythical time. Some claim to have emerged from the sun; others claim their origin in the moon; yet others in some distant ocean, or a mythical mountain or forest. What is astounding is that, in ancient India, the story of genesis was used as a basis for law governing inter-community relations. The hierarchy of the vocationally high and low implied in the *Purusha Sukta* was taken to mean a prescription with legal sanction. Thus, any attempt in thought, move, or gesture to change the hierarchy came to be seen as a sin against Purusha. Later, at whatever date the *Manusmriti* came into circulation, Purusha of the *Rigveda* was replaced by Brahma, a deity with whom Vedic lore would not have felt at ease.

The most critical account of the process through which the formulation articulated in the *Purusha Sukta* came to acquire an irreversible legal sanction is to be found in Dr B. R. Ambedkar's scholarly inquiry *Who Were the Shudras?* His thesis is that, initially, ancient India had only three *varnas*: Brahmin, Kshatriya, and Vaishya. The Shudras were not a *varna* but a community of the solar race. There was a continuous feud between the Shudra kings and the Brahmins. As a result of the enmity, the Brahmins refused to perform the *upanayana* ceremony for the Shudras. Due to the denial of the *upanayana*, the Shudras, who were equal to Kshatriyas, became socially degraded (Ambedkar, 1970). This long historical process resulted in the creation of the Shudras as a *varna*. Ambedkar's book is devoted to examining the veracity of this historical process. In his view, *upanayana* was made a privileged entitlement of the first three *varnas*, and denied to the fourth one. The concept of *upanayana* rests on the idea of the possibility of a second birth, though a metaphoric one. In the initial form of the *upanayana*, the ritual did not involve the wearing of a *yajnopavita*, or the sacred thread, around one's chest. This practice crept in later when post-Vedic society started reading the metaphoric as being literal. *Upanayana* was, in its initial days, a symbolic birth, that is, the second birth of a person to the life of both the mind and the body. It was, in its original form, a rite of initiation. Such rites exist in various civilizations in a variety of forms. The Brahminic denial of ordaining a young person with the *yajnopavita* or the denial to perform the ritual of *upanayana* came to mean that the possibility of a second birth was foreclosed in the case of the Shudras.

One of the abiding concerns of the *Manu Samhita* was how to steer clear of impious deeds by following the dos and don'ts in relation to the inter-*varna* interactions. All these prescriptions were heavily biased in favour of those who could perform the *upanayana* ritual, and against those who could not; and starkly severe to those who were denied the possibility of *upanayana* altogether. If the Shudras were denied the entitlement to the *upanayana* ritual, by a slight extension of the same logic, it meant that they were denied the entitlement to all other rituals. They were, thus, ritually exiled. If they had been denied the entitlement to rituals because they were supposed to have committed some lowly acts in a previous life, then by a more aggressive extension of that logic, they were also destined to engage in all manner of 'impure' work in their present life—work such as scavenging, cleaning, skinning, tanning, etc. Since this warped logic denied the possibility of their rebirth, they came to be despised as being less than human and at par with other animals. Therefore, they were treated as such, without any fear of the perpetrators gaining any spiritual demerits. Given that this kind of metaphysics got translated into social and legal practices, there was no possibility of creating a humane society. The argument for this was closed in India forever. As the higher *varnas* found the given social arrangement to their advantage, they kept resisting every reformist movement.

SECT FORMATION

After the eighth century, Indian history witnessed the rise of many sects. The early sects arose round the figures of Shiva and Shakti. They originated in the southern regions first. By the eleventh century, the rise of sects had become a widespread phenomenon in the subcontinent. By the end of the fifteenth century, many founders of such sects had already been accepted in public memory as divine figures. Since the idea of the avatar came to occupy centre stage in the dynamics of sect emergence, Krishna and Rama—the two heroes of the two pan-Indian epics—became cult figures for many of the sects. This entire movement highlighted the possibility of release for any individual, born high or low, negating the logic on which the *varna* system was based. The eighth to the eighteenth century is the period when *jati* became the main principle for social segregation in India. The *jatis* had no clear metaphysical basis. They were more an expression of difference in terms of language, region, occupation, cultivation practices, food habits, and skills. But these differences, once accepted, led to a particular *jati* formation, with its identity being invariably expressed in terms of the specific practice of worship. If the metaphysics based on the story of genesis was the basis for *varna* consolidation, the perception of difference leading to a metaphysical view was at the heart of the *jati* formation process. In one, metaphysics was the cause; in the other, it was the consequence, expressive of the desire of the non-Brahminical classes to be counted at par.

It is not surprising that when the colonial Europeans arrived in India, they found the social segmentation utterly confusing. During the seventeenth century, the Portuguese in India followed the practice of describing every community as a tribe. This term became somewhat less favoured when the British, French, and Portuguese started noticing the sharp distinctions between the dominating communities and the dominated communities in India. It was at this time that they began using the term caste for the higher classes. The difficulty of the Europeans continued throughout their colonial rule in India, for while they could more easily understand the linguistic, racial, and formal theological distribution of Indian society and the economic segregation of the different classes, the vast diversity of *jatis*, informal and non-institutional, eluded their anthropological grasp. They could not fathom how the *jati* consolidation worked; how within the overall framework of *varnas*, the *jatis* placed themselves in a defined social hierarchy; how endogamy and exogamy worked in these *jatis*; and what made a perfectly normal-looking human act appear criminal in the eyes of another given community. Besides, colonial scholars had no means of grasping the structural principles of sects which permitted multiple belief affiliations.

British colonial officers, well-meaning or otherwise, made repeated attempts at understanding the social and linguistic cartography of India. Most of these attempts were initiated in order to meet the demands of consolidating the government's authority, though that was not invariably the case. However, the inadequate understanding of the dialectic between religion and sect, *varna* and *jati*, language and script, often resulted in these attempts deepening the differences. A large number of Indians think that the largest number of languages spoken today is derived from Sanskrit, some from Tamil and some others in the Northeast from Sino-Tibetan or Tibet-Burmese origin. It is also known to anthropologists, linguists, and some tribal activists that we have languages of Austro-Asiatic derivation too. All Indians are keenly aware that Arabic and Persian have given to our languages a great wealth of words. Needless to add that they also recognize and experience, in their daily interactions, how the English language has contributed a substantial amount of new expressions and words to Indian languages. What is not known, except in small circles of archaeologists and scholars of ancient India, is that several Prakrits and Pali have contributed as significantly to our languages as have Sanskrit, Tamil, Arabic, Persian, and English.

FROM SANSKRIT-PRAKRITS TO THE BHASHAS

The amnesia about how significantly the Prakrits and, to an extent Pali, have contributed to all that India speaks and thinks is not of recent origin. It goes back in the past at

India: A Linguistic Civilization

least for a millennium. For most part of that long period of anonymity of Pali, the Prakrits have been active, but without recalling that the Prakrits were firmly wedded to the Pali language in ancient times dating nearly to the fifth century. Therefore, the knowledge of the language that was used for documenting the most central canonical Jain and Buddhist texts remained confined to a handful of initiated monks for centuries. Alas, Buddhism was banished in the first millennium CE from its country of birth, and the knowledge of Pali Buddhist texts remained alive in countries outside India such as Sri Lanka, Nepal, and Thailand. The many regional varieties of Prakrits continued their existence in transmuted form. Thus, from the tenth century CE onwards one variety of Prakrit developed as Gujarati, another as Bangla and Odia, and a third one as Marathi and Konkani, to mention but a few examples. During the period of the emergence of India's modern *bhashas* such as Sindhi, Kashmiri, Punjabi, Hindi, Marathi, Gujarati, Odia, Bangla, Nepali, and Assamiya, people had moved away from Sanskrit. While a small number of scholars continued to produce texts in Sanskrit through that period, most of the thinkers, saints and poets chose to turn to the Prakrit-based languages that had been emerging a thousand years before our time. A Marathi saint-poet of the fourteenth century put this sentiment in perspective when he asked, 'If Sanskrit is Dev-bhasha, made by gods, is Marathi made by thieves?' His predecessor Dnyanadeva said that Marathi is sweeter than nectar. In other words, by the beginning of the second millennium, Indians had moved beyond both Sanskrit and

Pali. Fortunately for the Pali language, it received a fresh impetus in Sri Lanka from Ratnamati, alias Ratnashrijnana (900–980 CE).

Towards the end of the eighteenth century, Sir William Jones's hypothesis drew all scholarly attention to the history of Sanskrit. Following William Jones's hypothesis, other scholars like Francis Whyte Ellis in 1816 and Robert Caldwell in 1856 pointed out that just as there was an Indo-Aryan language family, there was also a Dravidian language family. No scholar paid comparable attention to Pali and the Prakrits, and they were described in tentative and uncertain terms as offshoots of Sanskrit. Dharmanand Kosambi's (1876–1947) work in drawing attention to Pali was significant. A year-and-a-half after his death, the Constituent Assembly resolved to institute a separate schedule for languages in the Constitution. Sanskrit was included in it, though no Indians had used Sanskrit as a language of everyday life for more than a thousand years. The language in which Buddhist scriptures are written received no attention, despite the twentieth century revival of Buddhism in India.

To get an idea of how, many languages other than Sanskrit have contributed to India's linguistic composition, it may help to look at the current map of India. The languages of the Northeast are known to have descended neither from Sanskrit nor from Tamil. The languages in the South as well as in Goa, Maharashtra, Orissa, West Bengal, and Bihar are nurtured by either Prakrits or the ancient Tamil. In comparison, the areas that have languages coming straight from Sanskrit are fewer. The Prakrits served as the languages of the non-elites in ancient India since Sanskrit was primarily the language of the elite rulers and priestly classes. Commenting on the Sanskrit-Prakrit relation, Andrew Ollett states:

> Prakrit is the name of a literary language that was used from roughly the beginning of the Common Era. The word means 'common' (literally, 'of or relating to the basic character') and contrasts with 'Sanskrit', meaning 'refined'. It thus designates a language that according to the *Natyashastram* (*Treatise on Theatre*), is exactly the same as Sanskrit, but reversed, in so far as it lacks the quality of Sanskrit. Sanskrit and Prakrit are often mentioned together as a contrasting pair, and the two of them would be recognised as India's pre-eminent literary languages up until the emergence of vernacular literatures (Devy et al., 2023).

In sociological terms, the labour classes, the peasants, the subjugated castes, the tribal people, and women in India have Prakrits as their heritage languages. So far, no one in India has asked the question as to why Pali—the language of Buddhist and Jain cannons—has not been included in the Eighth Schedule of India's Constitution as was Sanskrit. Certainly, a considerable amount of additional research and investigation is necessary for us to know the exact role played by Pali in the making of India. Eminent contemporary scholar of Pali, Mahesh Deokar outlines the following questions related to Pali that are still awaiting in-depth scrutiny:

> What was the process of canonisation and what were the criteria of qualifying the canonical texts? Why does

there seem to have been no production of Pali texts between the third century BCE and the third century CE? (He mentions the *Milind-panho* as an exception to this observation.) What was the state of Pali during this period? How, if at all, did Pali interact with other Buddhist textual traditions, such as the Sanskrit and Gandhari, in this long period? What can we learn about the Pali canon by comparing it to related texts in Sanskrit, Gandhari and Chinese? What were the processes by which the Pali tradition was committed to writing in manuscript forms? Why was Pali revived systematically in Sri Lanka in the eleventh century CE and how? What was the state of Pali at that juncture of history? When scholars find answers to these questions, the history of Sanskrit may start looking much different from what it appears to be at present (Devy et al., 2023).

Sanskrit produced abundant philosophical, liturgical, and imaginative literature. So did Pali, Tamil, and the Prakrits. The radically different life values and philosophical concepts in these traditions of thought need to be seen as the cultural and intellectual outcome of the 'language-mix India'. It was the complex and elaborate processes of the language-mix, spread over nearly two millennia and more, that shaped India in a form and texture radically different than in which it was shaped from the beginning of human existence till the decline of the Indus Civilization. It superimposed on the previously valued notions of the earth, or the mother goddess, and the bull, the votive symbols of fertility, the concepts dominating the Sanskrit world of knowledge, *sunya*, nothingness, and *brahma*, the universal essence of being as the sum total of human existence.

THE INDIA OF LANGUAGE REBELLIONS
Cultural forms developed in classical India from the third to the tenth centuries started undergoing momentous changes at the beginning of the second millennium. The most fundamental of these was the emergence of new languages—*bhashas*—all over the Indian subcontinent. The new *bhashas* expressed regional and heterodox aspirations in protest against the hegemony of Sanskrit and the culture developed through that language—*sanskriti*. A similar movement occurred in the South with respect to Tamil, which, after a continuous history of two thousand years, branched into Telugu (eleventh century). Earlier, Kannada had already become an independent dialect of Tamil (fifth century). Nine hundred years later, Tamil and Kannada jointly gave birth to Malayalam (fourteenth century). In the North, the regional dialects known as *Apabhramsa* asserted themselves as independent languages. Consequently, the Middle Indo-Aryan dialects in the East split into Bangla and Odia (tenth century). Subsequently, Bangla gave birth to Assamiya (thirteenth century). The Northwestern dialect developed into Kashmiri (thirteenth century), Sindhi (fifteenth century), and Punjabi (fourteenth century). The western *Apabhramsa* of Middle Indo-Aryan distributed itself into Hindi (which till the beginning of the nineteenth century existed as several distinct dialects), Gujarati (eleventh century), and Marathi

(eleventh century). The Hindi family of dialects developed autonomy in the fourteenth century. It also interacted with Persian, which was spoken in India from the thirteenth to the nineteenth centuries, and Arabic, in use from the eleventh to the nineteenth centuries, and produced the cantonment language Urdu (thirteenth century), which later became a great literary language. The origin of some of these languages can be traced further back to earlier centuries. We are told that Gujarati and Marathi, for example, existed in rudimentary forms as found in stray inscriptions and isolated verses dating from the eighth century. Their known literary traditions, however, do not seem to emerge until a century or two after each language assumed a distinct identity. In any case, all *bhashas* had become literary languages by the end of the fifteenth century. The emergence and survival of mature literary traditions in so many languages is the greatest phenomenon in Indian cultural history.

The earliest prose work in Marathi is Mhaimbhat's *Leela Charitra* (completed in 1278). The earliest surviving poetic work is Mukundaraja's *Vivek Sindhu* (exact date disputed; he died in 1200); Jnanadeva's *Jnanesvari* (completed in 1290) was the first Marathi classic to be critically acclaimed. The Gujarati literary tradition was inaugurated by Hemachandra (1088–1173), poet-saint and grammarian, who lived about the mid-twelfth century. He was a poet, lexicographer, and theorist. His *Kavyanusasana* (completed in 1140) is considered to be a valuable contribution to Sanskrit poetics. The text was composed in Sanskrit and leaned more towards scholarly analysis rather than presenting original ideas.

The fact that Hemachandra brought the whole tradition of Sanskrit knowledge discourse to the threshold of Gujarati literary tradition is endorsed by his modern commentators. Like Hemachandra, Mukundaraja, considered to be the first Marathi poet, had an intimate knowledge of Sanskrit intellectual traditions. Marathi and Gujarati had the advantage of founding their own literary traditions upon intellectual developments in Sanskrit. Other *bhasha* literatures, too, had the benefit of contact with Sanskrit.

The emergence of *bhasha* literatures coincided with, even if it was not entirely caused by, a succession of Islamic rules in India. The Islamic rulers—Arabs, Turks, Mughals—brought with them new cultural currents to India, and provided these currents legitimacy through liberal political patronage. Their languages—Arabic and Persian, mainly, and Urdu which developed indigenously under their influence—brought new modes of writing poetry and music. This intimate contact with Islamic cultures created for the *bhasha* literatures new possibilities of continuous development. The tremendous wave of *Bhakti* poetry, which swept India across all linguistic boundaries and over an extended temporal span, selected its central symbolism, manifest in Krishna-bhakti, by no accident. Of course, Krishna-bhakti was not the only kind of devotionalism prevalent during that period. Poets like Tulsidas (1532–1623) in Hindi and Ramdas (1608–1681) in Marathi felt inspired to follow Rama. The Sufi poets wrote about an idealized feminine principle, and in Marathi a strong tradition of Datta-cult literature also emerged. However, it cannot be denied that the charismatic child god, Krishna, provided the main paradigm for devotionalism. During the *Bhakti* period, many local variations on Krishna-bhakti became popular in different regions of India. Various myths related to Krishna's life were enshrined in cults developed around the significant geographical centres, Vrindavan and Mathura. In Maharashtra, the local form of Krishna: Vitthal or Vithoba, was worshipped. It was around Vithoba, the god in Pandharpur, that the Warkari sect grew, and assimilated in its body of scriptures the poetry of Jnanadeva, Namadeva, Eknath and Tukaram, who were by far the greatest Marathi poets. In most *bhashas* the story of Krishna's life, and isolated episodes from it, particularly those that symbolized free play of libidinal and subconscious impulses, became a source of inspiration to poets. Numerous poems were written, for instance, on the romantic episode of Krishna's wedding with Rukmini. This tremendous upsurge of *Bhakti* literature was the visible index of complex but fundamental changes taking place in Indian society during the high tide of Islamic rule. *Bhakti* was not a movement restricted to any one area of life. It was a composite concept and a pervasive movement, which medieval India posed as an alternative to the hegemony of *marga* traditions and to the excessively sophisticated system of Sanskrit poetics.

Much of the literature of the pre-British *bhasha* period is still a living heritage in India. The poetry of Namadeva (1270–1350) and Tukaram (1598–1650) in Marathi, that of Narsinh Mehta (1408–80) and Akha (1615–1674) in Gujarati, of Kabir (1440–1518) and Surdas (1483–1567) in Hindi, of Guru Nanak (1469–1539) in Punjabi, and so on, has formed an inalienable part of the Indian consciousness. Tukaram, Mira, Kabir, and Basaveshwar, among others, have been some of the dream images of India's cultural unconscious. The common term used to describe the above-named pre-colonial poets is *Bhakti*, devotionalism, or saint poetry. The term covers a vast period extending from the last part of the thirteenth century (Jnanadeva) to the early part of the seventeenth century. The music, painting, dance, architecture, and poetry which emerged during this period form a glorious chapter in India's cultural history. Yet, no simple formula of the relationship between living cultural traditions and great social problems can explain the entire period satisfactorily. Rather, one encounters here a paradox difficult to explain. Side by side with Marathi poet Tukaram's (1598–1649) redefinition of the traditional Hindu world-view, one finds Jagannatha (1620–1665) concluding the long, tired line of poetics in Sanskrit. On the one hand we see the development of a genre of history writing like the Assamiya *Buranji*, and on the other, myth-making replacing in Hindi after a robust questioning of ethics in the preceding century by Mira (1498–1573) and Kabir (1440–1518). It was in the seventeenth century that Punjabi produced a great poet like Waris Shah (1722–1798), and Gujarati the equally great Premanand (1636–1714) and Akha (1591–1656); but the same period saw a rapid decline in Telugu literature in spite of ample patronage given to the arts in Andhra. The great Marathi poet Tukaram was Jagannatha's contemporary. So were two other major figures of the Marathi poetic tradition: Mukteshvar (late sixteenth century) and Ramdas

(1608–1681). While Jagannatha was composing verses on Mughal courtiers in the tired metres of Sanskrit, Tukaram had been creating a new social and spiritual discourse. Tukaram's vibrant and socially oriented poetry, written in a living language, contributed substantially to the growing Maratha nationalism. When we juxtapose Jagannatha with Tukaram, within their shared cultural context, it would be possible to formulate the following two questions:

1. What was the exact historical sequence of the decline of the Sanskrit universe of knowledge and the emergence of *bhasha* literatures?
2. What was the nature of the relation between the Great Tradition and the newly emerging little traditions, between the *marga* and *desis*?

EMERGENCE OF THE BHASHAS

A unique strategy evolved by the *bhasha* literatures to subvert the rigid conventions of over-stylized Sanskrit poetry, to confront the Brahminic monopoly of metaphysics and ethics, and assert the identity of regional aspirations, was the essence of *bhakti*. It brought with it a new social philosophy, metaphysics, and aesthetics. However, *bhakti* was a movement and not a philosophical system. It had its own dynamics, but it never attempted a systematic theorizing of the values it upheld. In reversing the established relation of hierarchy between the *marga* and the *desi* traditions, it rattled the bones of an already ossified society, and substantially changed its complexion.

At the centre of Vedic society was the concept of

vak (speech as an act and as abstraction) and its capacity to regulate the material universe. Similarly, during the late classical period, the philosophy of *Advaita Vedanta* was organized around the concepts of *sphota* and *dhvani* (explosion and suggestion of meaning, or meaning), especially in Sankara's (788 CE) *Brahmasutra-bhasya*. His pronouncement, *vacharambhananam vikaro* (knowing is seizing with speech) has been commented upon by innumerable Vedantins. *Sphota* was thus one of the most crucial concepts of Sankara's philosophy, which in turn was the most characteristic intellectual product of classical Hinduism. Like *vak* and *sphota* in the earlier millennia, *bhakti* came to occupy the centre stage of Indian culture for nearly five centuries—from the fourteenth to the eighteenth. However, both *vak* and *sphota* were products of the *marga* tradition, whereas *bhakti* originated in *desi* traditions of the *bhasha* literatures.

It has long been recognized that languages and regionalism have been interrelated in India, and that the relationships of any one region to Sanskrit on the one hand, and to its own *bhasha* on the other, have been different in nature. Sanskrit, used only for the purpose of higher pursuits ever since the language naturalized itself in India, was distributed all over the country, including those parts that were using Dravidian languages. It was spread horizontally in a sense, all over India, without taking strong roots in any specific region. During the Indo-Islamic centuries, the prestige of Sanskrit and its use were further undermined. Communication through Sanskrit, therefore, took place in extended geographic space but was confined to small pockets of communities surrounded by non-Sanskrit speakers. Sanskrit did not have the same speech culture as the *bhashas* had. In such a situation, the spoken Sanskrit word was perishing fast. The regional languages were 'living' languages, and communication through them was intended for a living and compact society.

During the age of classical Sanskrit literature, literary texts were passed on from generation to generation by committing them to memory. However, the texts were preserved in written form by periodically reproducing the manuscripts. With the advent of the *bhashas* these methods underwent a sociological as well as a technological change. The sociological change occurred because the class and caste structures came under heavy attack from new sectarian movements, which, reflected in *Bhakti* poetry, did not accept theological knowledge as a purely Brahminic monopoly. Many non-Brahmins started preaching their own realization of religious knowledge, through their poetry. In Marathi, Namdev (1270–1350) was a tailor by caste. He was surrounded by Gora Kumbhar, a potter (1267–1317), Savata, a *mali* or a gardener (1250–1295), Chokhamela, a Mahar (1273–1338), Sena Nhavi, a barber, and Janabai, a Matang (1258–1350). Many of these poets were illiterate and they composed poems for the benefit of the illiterate classes. Therefore, they preferred 'publishing' the poems as oral compositions rather than as written texts. They sang their poems to large gatherings in places of pilgrimage or in the streets. The function of the text, and its place in the literary culture, had changed. The technological change came with the use of paper for writing. Paper was introduced in India by the twelfth century. By the early fourteenth century, during the reign of Muhammad bin Tughlaq (1325–1351), India was exporting paper and books to Iran and other Islamic nations. It was now possible to make copies of texts easily, as writing with ink on paper was easier than with herbal dyes on leaves. The new technology was probably used more by the elite Sanskrit writers whose appeal was limited to a small number of readers. It widened the gap that already existed between elite poetry and popular poetry.

Before the introduction of paper as a literary technology, the distinction between elite literature and folk literature was based on the clear criteria of written poetry and oral poetry. The poetry of *bhashas* was neither entirely written nor entirely oral. It was certainly consciously composed, and though many poets continued to operate orally, some actually wrote down their own verse. Given the long entanglement of the Sanskrit language with the Brahminical social order, *bhasha* poetry could not completely replace either the Sanskrit written poetry or the regional folk poetry. It was a cross between the two, and was an altogether new category of poetry.

The development of *Bhakti* poetry was a natural consequence of the emergence of the *bhasha* literatures. *Bhakti* unleashed an emotionalism which classical Indian literature had held under the strict control of conventions and rigidly defined social ethics. In revolting against them, and in turning to an unrestrained emotionalism, *Bhakti* made itself incapable of developing intellectual systems founded on rational thought. It had a revolutionary social and literary drive which manifested in symbolism and mysticism, but could not find the rational strength necessary to formulate an intellectual discourse. It tried every kind of experimentation with style and diction, and replaced every established convention of poetry, but it never tried to formulate a statement of the new conventions of poetry. The movement did not initiate a new theory of literature, primarily due to a breakdown in the intricate network of the *marga* and *desi* traditions. Sociologically, devotional poetry was a challenge posed by the oppressed classes to the Brahminical monopoly of cultural and scriptural knowledge. The challenge, however, did not make a dent in the formal system of knowledge transmission. The prevalent patterns of patronage intensified this class war in literature. The political structures prevalent during the *Bhakti* centuries were feudalistic. Though change of regimes was a constant feature of the political history of this period, dissent at the popular level was equally dreaded by all rulers. *Bhakti* literature, therefore, was not welcomed by the class capable of providing political patronage to literature. It would be more appropriate, perhaps, to say that the *marga* tradition accepted only the theological content of *Bhakti*, neglecting its rebellious spirituality. Hence, the ruling classes continued to provide uninterrupted patronage to Sanskrit-based formal education all through the middle centuries. Persian and Arabic were added to Sanskrit when the patronage was provided by the Islamic rulers. In other words, formal education belonged to *marga*, while the experience of life's complexities was perceived and articulated through *desi* idiolects (Devy, 1992).

India: A Linguistic Civilization

THE COLONIAL RESPONSE TO LANGUAGE DIVERSITY

The term 'civilization' is no longer a term that historians, ethnographers or archaeologists use with any great fondness. It gained currency primarily in Europe as a cultural-history description when Edward Gibbons (1737–1794) published his six volumes, *History of the Decline and Fall of the Roman Empire*, between 1776 and 1788. His theme was civilization and its destruction caused by barbaric enemies. He wrote, 'After a diligent inquiry, I can discern four principal causes of the ruin of Rome, which continued to operate in a period of more than a thousand years: i. injuries of time and nature; ii. hostile attacks of the Barbarians and Christians; iii. use and abuse of the materials; and, iv. domestic quarrels of the Romans.' The success of his work was such that there was hardly anyone in England with any claim to education, class, and social distinction who had not read the copious tomes produced by Gibbons. It was as if to read Gibbons was to be civilized. It would be surprising, therefore, if Sir William Jones (1746–1794)—referred to as 'Sir' in order to distinguish him from his famous mathematician father, who too was named William Jones (1675–1749)—would not have read it. Sir William founded the Asiatic Society in Calcutta (now Kolkata) in 1784 and presented his most important observation to the world in 1786, well received in Europe in the heydays of Gibbons's history. The term 'civilization' was implicit, though not foregrounded, in William Jones's formulation related to historical linguistics. His hypothesis was about ancient relationships between various European and Asian languages, or the 'Indo-European' languages. In his *Third Anniversary Discourse* (1786) to the Asiatic Society, he suggested that Sanskrit, Greek, and Latin languages had a common root, and that indeed they may all be related, in turn, to Gothic and the Celtic languages, as well as to Persian, indicating the existence of an older language, no longer in existence in his time, a 'proto-Indo-European language'. Jones concluded that all these had probably developed from a common source.

Jones's well-founded hypothesis and the work of his eminent scholar colleagues, such as Charles Wilkins (1749–1836), Nathaniel Halhed (1751–1830), Alexander Hamilton (1757–1804), and James Prinsep (1799–1840), provided Indians of their time a new thread to connect themselves with ancient India. Previously, the connection was through myths, legends and epics. Jones's hypothesis opened up a path for the late eighteenth century India to approach its remote past. His Asiatic Society colleagues and successive generations of European scholars in Calcutta, Madras (now Chennai), Bombay (now Mumbai), and other stations of the East India Company continued to produce a new and scientific knowledge about Indian geology, geography, society, literature, language, religion, arts, and possibly every conceivable area of knowledge. Given the political dominance of the British during the nineteenth century, the body of knowledge produced by the European Indologists became quite influential. Besides, the industry of these Indological scholars was remarkable. Here is, as a sample, an inventory of the more important work produced by members of the Bombay Literary Society (later renamed Asiatic Society of Mumbai).

Sir James Mackintosh (1765–1832), founded the Literary Society of Bombay in 1804 and created a platform for scholarly activities. He authored several books on history, politics, and ethics. William Erskine (1773–1852), author of the monumental *A History of India under the Two First Sovereigns of the House of Taimur, Baber and Humayun* (1854), opened a new perspective on the medieval Indian history. He founded the Literary Society of Bombay. Vans Kennedy, a major general in the Company Army, had command over twelve languages and produced, apart from several short papers, a Marathi-English Dictionary. John Briggs (1785–1875), a scholar of eastern languages, history and science, wrote several important books, the most well-known of his works being the English translation of Ferishta's *Tarikh-i-Ferishta*. He also penned the *History of the Rise of Mahomedan Power in India till the Year 1612* (1829). Captain James MacMurdo (1785–1820), though not a scholar, provided documentation for other works on historiography of Gujarat, Kathiawad, Kutch, and Sindh. William Henry Sykes (1790–1872), an ornithologist and naturalist, compiled useful catalogues on the life and culture of western India. George Buist (1805–1860), editor of *Bombay Times*, the precursor of the *Times of India*, shaped the prose style for journalism, which in turn had a profound impact on the prose literature in Marathi and Gujarati. William Edward Frere (1811–1880), a numismatist and active member of the Bombay Geographical Society, set the Bibliotheca Orientalis with the intention of collecting manuscripts in Sanskrit, Gujarati, Marathi, Zend, Pahlavi, and many other languages. Henry John Carter

(1813–1895) undertook the study of geology as well as of the Indian Ocean. His publications contributed to a variety of disciplines, including Zoology, Marine Science, Geology, and Natural Science. Philip Anderson (1816–1857), a clergyman by profession, provided an insightful analysis of the British rule in India in his book *English in Western India* (1856). Alexander Kinloch Forbes (1821–1865), wrote the *Ras Mala* (1856), on the history and culture of Gujarat. He founded three institutions, still in existence: Gujarat Vernacular Society at Ahmedabad, Andrews Library at Surat, and the Gujarati Sabha (later renamed as the Forbes Gujarati Sabha) at Bombay. All three had a profound impact on the nineteenth century intellectual life in Gujarat. Peter Peterson (1847–1899) was the last European professor of Oriental Languages at the Elphinstone College in Bombay. John Faithfull Fleet (1848–1917) was an excellent scholar of Sanskrit as well as Kannada and authored an important history of medieval Karnataka. His work on epigraphs established a scientific model for study of Indian epigraphs. Under the influence of the Orientalist scholars, a new knowledge of India emerged for the contemporary Indians, and a new philosophy of historical linguistics developed in Germany and France which started classifying languages into language families. Initially, it was claimed that all Indian languages had grown out of Sanskrit. Gradually, the Dravidic language family, the source of which was Tamil, was proposed by Robert Caldwell in 1856.

Since the times of Sir William Jones, major attempts have been made to propose and formulate conceptual categories for describing the linguistic and cultural diversity and knowledge traditions in India. The corresponding process of decolonization, has also spurred efforts to align traditional knowledge with the colonial production of knowledge within the context of Western modernity. While the clash, as well as collaboration, between what is seen as knowledge compatible with the Western cognitive categories and knowledge traditions rooted in the lives of predominantly oral communities, continue to occupy the imaginative transactions in India, the mainstream institutions of knowledge—such as schools, universities, hospitals, courts, etc.—have acquired forms that often leave out the complexities involved in the 'great transition of civilization in the Indian sub-continent'. This situation poses an intellectual challenge that thinkers in the twenty-first century need to negotiate. Probably, the most important among the cognitive categories that continue to carry traces of this 'transition in civilization' belong to the field of creative expression in language and the one related to language description.

The last large-scale language survey was carried out by George Abraham Grierson (1851–1941), a linguist from Ireland. Over the century since Grierson completed the monumental and pioneering work, it has acquired the status of a permanent touchstone in relation to any sociolinguistic discussion of languages in India. The most striking feature of Grierson's Survey (1903-28/2006) is the silent spaces in them. Even at the beginning of the twentieth century, which was Grierson's time, one notices through his account the beginning of a slow demise for nearly 165 out of the 179 languages—the languages not in print in his time—that he documented and described. There is as yet no full-scale comparison between Grierson's 'linguistic discoveries of India' with a similar discovery by his eminent predecessor Sir William Jones. Jones was excited about the presence of different languages in India, though of course he had no way of knowing how many of them existed in his time. In contrast, Grierson's description had no such 'eureka' about it. When one wades through the Grierson volumes, one returns home with the impression that the languages reported in them are in most part the rustic varieties, fit only for housing childish songs and materials good enough for folklorists subservient to anthropology. As against the less than 200 languages that he described, he had over 500 dialects to describe. The arithmetic of the great work is indicative of its essential bias. Perhaps, the beginning of it was embedded in the work of William Jones and the other scholars of his generation who collectively created Indology as a field of knowledge, despite there being apparent euphoria in discovering India as an unknown continent of civilization.

The intellectual industry of Indology was devoted to describing India in every aspect of its remote past and its contemporary situation. However, the knowledge forms developed in ancient and medieval India did not find favour with the European scholars engaged in the literary and linguistic archaeology of India. Within the field of Linguistics, India had produced a series of significant positions, beginning with Panini's *Ashtadhyayi,* and going through, to name but a few, Katyayana, Patanjali and Bhartrihari, to Anandavardhana's *Dhvanyaloka*. The theories such as *vyakarana*, *sphota* and *dhvani* were indeed important scientific and philosophical ways of looking at sounds, words, sentences and meaning. For the European Indologists, these and other texts like them were material to rediscover, study and translate, but not the texts that could be imbibed, assimilated with modern scientific thinking, and used as the conceptual framework for narrating India to the rest of the nineteenth-century world.

Panini's search was for finding out the roots of words (*dhatu*) by isolating the original and its affixes (*pratyaya*) or inflections. He drew up rules for word formation using a small number of root words and analysing their manifold transformations caused by affixes and inflections. Bhartrihari had demonstrated how meaning of a sentence is caused through *sphota*, which, in his formulation, brings the phonetic body of words together with the semantic references evoked by those words in the moment of realization of the intent. Anandavardhana had offered elaborate analysis of various levels or orders of expressed meaning as well as nascent meaning-intentions in his theory of *dhvani*. The orientation of the Indian tradition of scholarship in Linguistics was primarily structural and analytical. William Jones was looking at the evolution and transformation of language-bodies, through a genetic prism. Besides, the political context of scholarship of the European Indologists was clearly averse to granting Indian traditions of thought the prerogative of theorising. Therefore, the *Vedangas*, *Vyakaranas*, and *Niruktas* which constituted Linguistics in Sanskrit were not of any great interest to the Historical Linguistics of the late eighteenth and early nineteenth century European scholars. William Jones's hypothesis on the ancient relatedness of languages of Europe and Asia had far-reaching impact on language studies in Europe. The Historical and Comparative Linguistics ruled the field for more than a century; and along its way, it also gave rise to a fraudulent claim by Nazi Germany about Aryan supremacy. The idea of Language Family, analogous to the Zoological family tree was applied to languages, which are non-biological and purely sociological systems.

In the pre-colonial epistemologies of language, hierarchy in terms of a standard and dialect was not common. Language diversity was an accepted fact of life. Literary artists could use several languages within a single composition, and their audience accepted the practice as normal. Great works like the epic Mahabharata continued to exist in several versions handed down through a number of different languages almost till the beginning of the twentieth century (Deshpande, 1978). When literary critics theorized, they took into account literature in numerous languages. Matanga's medieval compendium of styles, *Brihad-deshi*, is an outstanding example of criticism arising out of the principle that language diversity is normal (Devy, 1991).

During the colonial times, many of India's languages were brought into the print medium. It is not that previously the knowledge of writing was absent. Scripts were already used; paper too was used as a means of reproducing written texts. However, despite being written, texts had been mainly circulating orally. The print technology diminished the existing oral traditions. New norms of literature were introduced, privileging the written over the oral, and introducing the concept that a literary text needed to be essentially monolingual. These ideas, and the power relation prevailing in the colonial context, started affecting the stock of languages in India. The languages that had not been placed within the print technology came to be seen as inferior languages. After Independence, the Indian states were created on the basis of languages. If a language had a script, and if the language had printed literature in it, it was given a separate state within the Union of India. Languages that did not have printed literature, even though they had a rich tradition of oral literature, were not considered. Further, the state official language was used as a medium of primary and high school education within a given state. A special Schedule of Languages (the Eighth Schedule) was created within the Indian Constitution.

For most part of India's long history, for various regions in the subcontinent, multilingualism remained a natural cultural condition. Therefore, when the spirit of nationalism started developing in India, the idea of forming a single-language nation never crept into the thinking of any of the Indian nationalists, despite the differences between the ideological positions of the leaders during the freedom struggle. India as seen by them was already a single nation with many languages and also going to continue being one. The long and involved discussions in the Constituent Assembly from 1946 to 1949 provide ample testimony to the general acceptance of the idea of India as a nation with many languages. However, the Constituent Assembly had to resolve the contradiction between the astronomically large numbers of languages—of which it knew through Grierson's Survey—and the need for a nationally shared language of communication. The Constituent Assembly debates on this issue remained fairly inconclusive, resulting in the adoption of the special Schedule of Languages, the Eighth Schedule of the Constitution (Sarangi, 2009). After Independence, language diversity received a constitutional validity when the Constituent Assembly decided, after elaborate debate and discussion, to introduce the Eighth Schedule containing fourteen languages as deserving of recognition. The expanded list now consists of twenty-two languages. Nearly thirty languages are hoping to be included in it, if not the several hundred languages of Adivasis and nomadic communities, as also the languages of the Northeast and the coastal communities. While nationalism was spelt out in Europe during the nineteenth century in terms of linguistic unity, in India, speakers of these hundreds of different languages accepted to belong to a single nation because the Constitution had promised them the freedom of expression, making it mandatory on the state to encourage languages 'without harming other languages'. For millennia, Indians have cultivated a multilingual mindset, integrating it into their daily lives and environment. The national anthem they sing with such great pride describes India primarily in terms of some of its language communities, speakers of the Punjabi, Sindhi, Gujarati, Marathi, Dravidian languages, Odia, and Bangla. Clearly, Indians understand that their unity as a nation doesn't hinge on speaking a single language, nor does it falter despite their rich linguistic diversity; rather, it thrives precisely because of the multitude of languages they embrace. It was precisely for this reason that, soon after Independence, the union government set the State Reorganisation Commission and created linguistic states. It was Sir Herbert Risley (1851–1911), then the Home Secretary, who wrote to the Bengal government in 1903 introducing language as a divisive principle. As a result, Bengal was proposed to be partitioned in 1905 into East Bengal and West Bengal. When the idea of using language as the defining principle for demarcating provinces appeared in the Congress Session of 1917, Annie Besant strongly opposed it. A decade later, in its Nagpur Session in 1927, the Congress accepted the idea of linguistic distribution of the states.

While Jawaharlal Nehru accepted the principle, and the Linguistic Provinces Commission was set up in 1948, he cautioned against language becoming a threat to India's national unity. During the early 1950s, Andhra Pradesh became the first such linguistic state to be created in the wake of a violent popular agitation. In 1953, the State Reorganisation Commission was set up; however, two years later, Nehru was still trying to understand how the USSR had implemented this principle, and thus S. G. Barve was deputed to the USSR to study the Russian experience. That year, assured by the USSR experience, fourteen states and nine union territories were created. In the 1960s, Punjab was created, as a result of the agitation led by Sant Fateh Singh (1911–1967) and Master Tara Singh (1885–1967), and during the 1970s the Northeastern states were created. The process of creation of smaller states, making language as the central part of the arguments for creating them, has continued in India ever since Independence. The most recent instance of this process has been the agitation for creating a separate Telangana, the demand for a separate Vidarbha state and the splitting up of Uttar Pradesh into four zones. The entire process indicates clearly that India accepted the nineteenth-century ideas of nationalism as the basis of the Indian freedom struggle without accepting the idea of 'a nation as a linguistic singular', and though the Constituent Assembly debates displayed abundant respect for the idea of India as 'a linguistically plural nation', and language identity has played an important role in shaping the process of restructuring states (Schwartzberg, 2009).Implicit in the process is the flawed logic that every language that has a script, or has entered print technology and therefore has produced some of its literature in print, needs to assert its identity by aspiring to form a state within the 'nation as a language plural'. Probably, this insistence will continue to create political upheavals and mass movements till we realize that the hierarchy of languages based on the idea of writing as inherently superior to speech is neither linguistically scientific nor historically valid. This too would be a way of decolonizing knowledge and recovering the self.

LANGUAGE FAMILIES, LINGUISTIC AREA, AND LINGUISTIC CIVILIZATION

It has become an established disciplinary method to classify every known language in terms of its family affiliation. Languages that defy such classification are slotted into the category of isolates. The 2019 count of Language Families and Language Isolates in the world by Lyle Campbell indicates 406 such families and isolates (Campbell, 2019). One is not sure if the reports on ancient migrations offered by recent studies in Genetics corroborate the Language Family distribution as a theoretically valid position. Not fully satisfied with the classification in terms of families, the Russian linguist N. S. Trubetzkoy developed the concept of 'Language Area'. This English term is not what he used. His conceptual framework was used by Bernard Bloch, Roman Jakobson, Franz Boas, and Edward Sapir. It was applied by M. B. Emeneau in 1953 to explain the mutual influence of various Indian languages which are closely connected. The term used by Emeneau to describe the collective of languages, not belonging to the same language family but which have acquired common features is 'Language Area' ('area' not to be misunderstood as description of territorial space but as semantic space). In the essay proposing India as 'a Linguistic Area,' Emeneau points to features that exist in Gondi, Sanskrit, and Dravidic languages but which other branches of Indo-European languages do not possess. He further states:

> The use of classifiers can be added to those other linguistic traits (previously discussed) which establish India as one linguistic area for historical study. The evidence is at least as clear-cut as any that has been advanced in the establishment of a linguistic area in any part of the world, and in fact a good deal more so than much that has been offered. It is to be hoped that it will not be neglected henceforth when the question

is raised whether linguistic features, especially those of morphology and syntax, can diffuse across genetic boundaries. Some of the features presented here are, it seems to me, as 'profound' as we could wish to find (if we must attempt to apply Sapir's value criteria). Certainly the end result of the borrowings is that the languages of the two families, Indo-Aryan and Dravidian, seem in many respects more akin to one another than Indo-Aryan does to the other Indo-European languages. In another place I adumbrate an attempt to include the linguistic area India in the larger linguistic area of East, South-east, and South Asia. The evidence so far found concerns the use of classifiers and makes it at least possible that this trait reached the Indo-Aryan languages of the Magadhan area from Southeast Asia; but the demonstration of this is not as clear as that of the relationships within India and need not be given here to obscure the clear outlines of the matter.

Sprachbund or Linguistic Area, thus, works more efficiently as a description of the collective of Indian languages from different language families. Indian linguists have often based their observations about the unusually high percentage of shared vocabularies and some grammatical features of different Indian languages. However, while the concept of 'Area' works efficiently for a synchronic depiction of a language-collective and capturing its structural attributes, the vast range of languages in India and their exceedingly complex history, individually as well as collectively, calls for a rethink on the issue.

India: A Linguistic Civilization

THE UNCERTAIN LANGUAGE COUNTS

The story of Indian languages is extremely complex and has an epic span. The number of languages that have existed in the subcontinent in the past eras and the languages that are currently in existence—all put together—is far too large to admit any single and cohesive description. The extent of time over which some of those languages have been in use, without any radical break, too, is unusually large. Besides, it is just impossible to determine precise originary points for the language story of India. A further complication arises out of major perspective shifts in India's intellectual history on *how* languages are described. Panini (fourth century BCE), acknowledged as one of the all-time greats of linguists, had proposed in his *Ashtadhyayi* a certain way of analysing and describing languages. His language analysis had a profound impact on the Indian understanding of words and their interrelations. Twenty-two centuries after him, William Jones introduced another narrative for Indian languages. His classification, too, had an equally profound impact on how today's India views languages. So completely different are the epistemic foundations of the two perspectives, that reconciling the two has neither been attempted nor will it ever be possible.

There was human habitation in India for thousands of years prior to the emergence of Sanskrit, and it is known that various languages existed, but we have no record of those languages which can help to reconstruct the entire linguistic past. The earliest records of oral texts date to about thirty-five centuries BP, and the earliest records of writing date to twenty-four centuries BP (Devy et al., 2023). While scripts had been in use in other parts of Asia and west of India for fifty centuries BP, why the neighbouring Indian subcontinent took so long to get into lexical modes of expression is not yet fully investigated. The yet non-deciphered sign system of the Indus Valley civilization makes any historical narrative of Indian languages incomplete and tentative (Robinson, 2009). Writing originated in India some twenty-four centuries BP in the form of inscriptions and hand-written manuscripts. The writing culture was completely transformed when paper came into use about ten centuries BP, and it experienced another profound shift two centuries BP with the advent of printing of the first few Indian languages. We still do not have any conclusive knowledge of the remote-ancient past of Tamil and several other indigenous languages in existence during the second millennium BC in the Eastern parts of India. We know that at a somewhat uncertain point in time during the phase of India's transformation from a hunter-gatherer society to a pastoral society, a branch of the remote-ancient Dravidic spread to the North and another to the Northwest. Nevertheless, the precise timing remains unknown. Finally, it is still a mystery as to when exactly the languages described in Historical Linguistics as 'Isolates'—the Nehali spoken in Maharashtra's Buldhana district is an instance—emerged locally or arrived in their present location (Devy et al., 2023). These are only some of the difficulties in presenting a clear historical picture of the origin, rise, and transformation of languages.

There are similar challenges when we turn to the sociology of Indian languages. Archaeological and historical researches during the last two centuries have made it possible for us to know something about the complex linguistic transitions and migrations that took place over the last five millennia, roughly from the early Harappan times to our time (Joseph, 2018). During this long period, the Indian subcontinent accepted language legacies as distinct as the Avestan of the Zoroastrians, the Austro-Asiatic of the Pacific, the Tibeto-Burman of the East and the Northeast Asia. The Indic (or the Indo-Aryan) languages in the Northern states together with the Dravidic languages in the South, and the Tibeto-Burman languages in the Northeast, each with a great variety of sub-branches, make for the larger bulk of the Indian languages. Throughout the known history of the subcontinent, there has been an active exchange and cultural osmosis between the indigenous languages and the migratory languages, producing, in the process, great literature in many tongues. In the past, Sanskrit and Persian had acquired currency over considerably extensive geographical areas of the subcontinent. Yet, the local languages—the Prakrits and *Apabhramsas* (in the case of Sanskrit) and *desi-bhashas* (in the case of Persian)—continued to thrive (Deshpande, 1993). Over time, they gained greater currency and, in various amalgamated forms, overshadowed the supra-languages. The intimate love-hate relationship between Indian languages and the English language over the last two centuries is developing precisely along the same trajectory.

However, any neat separation of a given language from its surrounding languages, in theory, does not accurately reflect the ground reality of the existing languages. In order to get a picture of that, one must look into the figures provided by the census. These figures show that the languages listed in the Eighth Schedule have a much larger number of speakers than those not included. The only exception to this is English. This increase is caused not only by the general population growth in different linguistic states, but also by the decline of the languages not included in the Schedule. The decline is natural (and probably expected by the policy-makers), because the facilities provided for language education are mainly for the languages included in the Eighth Schedule. In the years to come, the other languages—mostly spoken by Adivasi communities and those belonging to the Austro-Asiatic family and the Tibeto-Burman family—may disappear altogether as a demographic indicator. That is to say that while the diction and the syntax patterns of these languages will no doubt survive, there may be a greater assimilation of these in the main languages of India. Whether this is desirable or not is a question that not only the cultural anthropologists, but all of us, have to answer. As for the main languages, the picture of their development is a mixed one. On the one hand, there is an unprecedented growth in the printed materials in these languages, and naturally so, given the multiplication of the print capitalism and digital technology from the nineteenth century till now; on the other hand, the English language has come up as the major adversary to these languages. Many members of the class which, during the nineteenth century, advocated the cause of the major Indian languages have turned to English as a vehicle for their economic betterment. As such, there has been a sharp decline in the number of readers of literature in Indian languages in cities and semi-urban areas.

Yet, there is another contrary element in the scene. The phenomenal spread of formal education in India's vast rural areas has created a new generation of readers and authors of Indian languages. In the process, new dialect varieties have entered the mainstream of Indian languages. The figures entered in the successive census reports under the category of mother tongues seem to indicate that Hindi is now claimed as the mother tongue by almost one in every three Indians. However, it is necessary to bear in mind that what is counted as Hindi is, in reality, a group of a large number of dialects, regional varieties and sub-languages. Hindi was claimed as the mother tongue by 208 million of the population in 1971, and by 264 million in 1981. This rise in number almost equals the total of Gujarati speakers (55million). As against Hindi which is the most widely spoken language in India, Sindhi, Nepali, Konkani, Manipuri, Kashmiri, and Sanskrit, which are some other languages listed in the schedule, together do not have more than eighty million speakers. Leaving these two uneven ends of the spectrum, the remaining eleven languages taken together (Assamese, Bengali, Gujarati, Malayalam, Marathi, Kannada, Odia, Punjabi, Tamil, Telugu, and Urdu) are spoken by almost half the population of India. Thus, these figures clearly show that there is a five-fold structure of Indian languages in terms of development. At the top are Hindi and English as rapidly-growing languages. Next in order, come the other major literary languages such as Bengali, Odia, Marathi, Tamil, Kannada, Punjabi, etc. Though the census lists Urdu in this group, the precise relation between Urdu and Hindi needs to be investigated in order to decide the distinction between their identities. After this is the group of major languages with a relatively smaller number of speakers—languages such as Sindhi, Manipuri, Konkani, etc. At the tail end of this structure are found two other groups: first, a group of languages that are not recognized as separate from the main language though there is some justification for that recognition. These include languages like Tulu, Kachchi, Ahirani, Marwadi, etc. In the second group are the languages of Adivasi communities and nomadic communities. A language like Bhantu, which is spoken by the Kanjara, Sansis, Chharas, and such other semi-nomadic groups, or Bhili, which is spoken by nearly three million, stand no chance of development because there are likely to be no schools or colleges teaching these languages, and no printing will ever be attempted in them. Thus, in this five-fold structure, the languages on the higher rungs are developed at the cost of languages on the lower rungs.

Linguists no longer prefer to discuss Indian languages in terms of distinct linguistic families; they have moved to describing the vast multitude of Indian languages as 'a linguistic area' having a far greater mutual intelligibility between a language and its surrounding languages than in most other parts of the world. Languages in India stand out not just by their great diversity but also as being an unmistakable key to its cultural tensions, social stratification as well as social transformation. Going by the estimates put forward by UNESCO and *Ethnologue*, there are about 7,000 living languages in the world. Of these, about 12 per cent are spoken in India. One should add that there is no decisive figure for the living Indian languages still available. The 2011 census had listed 1,369 'mother tongues'; but every 'label'—name of a mother tongue as entered by people during the census—is not necessarily a 'language'. In fact, successive governments have been trying to minimize the figures by introducing absurd methods for language count. The People's Linguistic Survey of India (2010–2013) reported 780 languages, with the caveat that the PLSI may have missed on some seventy languages. So, one can assume that there are about 850 living languages in the country. What is most remarkable about this vast diversity is that in any given period in the past, we had a similar diversity.

When Sanskrit arrived in India thirty-five centuries ago, there already were languages which were later identified as Prakrits and ancient Dravidian. Besides, wherever our ancient ancestors had struck roots, the 'population knots' formed by them had given rise to local languages. When Panini formulated his system of grammar twenty-five centuries BP, he mentioned not just one but numerous language varieties. Throughout the first millennium, works like Matanga's *Brhaddesi* and Kuntaka's *Vakrokti-Jivita* were built round the idea of many language varieties, and in plays of Kalidasa and Bhavabhuti, characters are seen using several languages within a single scene. During the first millennium,

Al Biruni, as well as Amir Khusrow, again reminded that to be Indian means to be speaking many languages. In the past, neither Sanskrit nor Persian, despite their metaphysical and material might, were able to replace regional and sub-national languages. The Prakrits continued to exist, though Sanskrit declined. Modern Indian languages of the areas ruled by Persian-speaking rulers continued, while Persian all but disappeared. The colonial rule succeeded in imposing a common legal framework over the entire geographical span we call India; however, despite Macaulay's education policy, imposing a single language had not been dreamed of by the rulers. India, whatever its protean being, is a linguistic civilization, and India's linguistic diversity is its perennial civilizational characteristic, its gene, its most essential epistemic attribute.

2

LANGUAGE AND THE STATE

THE NATION AND ITS LANGUAGES
The English language drew the term 'nation', during its historical phase known as Middle English, from the Latin root *'nationem'* signifying birth and ancestry. In its semantic trajectory within the English language, 'nation' was initially rooted in the idea of 'belonging to a geographical area or location'. It decidedly referred to an area, territory, and the people who inhabited it. The idea that a nation should ideally have a single language that will keep the people bound together was added to its range of signification during the early nineteenth century. This was the time when a new kind of longing for the past was emerging among the European painters and poets as a result of the devastation of the countryside due to rapid industrialization. In that mood of nostalgia, ancient poets (Homer and Aeschylus, in particular) began to be described as *vates* or prophets and language—more particularly, 'the original' language—as a spiritually potent agency of human liberation.

For instance, P. B. Shelley (1792–1822), in his essay, *A Defense of Poetry* (1821), lauds poetic language as a means of providing 'harmony and unity' to the prophetic vision of poets. This was precisely the time when the struggle for creating a united Italy had started. The unscientific association between a given language and a given people as 'nation' started emerging during this post-Napoleon era of European politics. By the time Germany emerged as a nation during the 1860s, the idea that, in addition to a shared history and a 'cohesive people', a common language too became an essential feature of a nation. With language, there were other features of intangible culture and history that got added to the prevalent meanings of the word 'nation'. The Irish Home Rule League decidedly revolved around Catholic Christianity; and in Spain and Germany, musical heritage and metaphysical philosophy too came to be part of their idea of nationhood.

There is no doubt that the Indian struggle for national independence was influenced by all these varieties of meaning associated with the term 'nation'. Towards the turn of the century, some of the influential leaders of public opinion in India had started visualizing the 'nation' for anchoring the complex economic and political struggle towards independence. Lokmanya Tilak (1856–1920) and Sri Aurobindo (1872–1950) tried to base it on what they thought were the foundations of Indian culture, and they tried to describe the nature of that foundation by harking back to India's ancient past. It is true that for over a century, since Sir William Jones launched the Asiatic Society as an enterprise in cultural archaeology, a lot of that past had been episodically described. Yet, in the work of European Indologists, the break in Indian tradition was taken as a non-negotiable of India's past.

In the works of nationalist leaders, the main thesis was based on the twin principles of the longevity and continuity of Indian culture. However, as events shaped, following the First World War, the idea of nation in Indian politics went through a significant shift. Just as the Home Rule League, catalysed in India by Annie Besant of Irish origin, was sidestepped, so was quietly dropped the idea of the Aryan past in the face of the rise of Fascism in Europe. Hence, in the 1920s, public figures in India had to engage with the language issue in the context of the possible formation of India as a free nation.

The first major manifestation of the collective thinking on this issue was the Congress resolution on setting up of linguistic states (1927) which was a clear acceptance of the need to preserve linguistic identities of the territories that would eventually join the nation. Previously, the Congress had set up its provincial committees along linguistic lines, and after 1927, the election manifestos of the Congress often included preservation of multiple linguistic identities as one of its obligations. By this time, the eleven volumes of George Grierson's massive *Linguistic Survey of India* had been published; and it was well known to opinion-makers that India had, at the beginning of the twentieth century, an amazing wealth of languages. Grierson had detailed 179 languages and several hundred others considered by him as 'dialects'.

Debates in the Constituent Assembly were, therefore, mindful of the need to imagine India as a nation with many languages and the dangers in straitjacketing it within a monolingual or bilingual administrative apparatus. Not surprisingly, the Constitution made space for fourteen languages in its Eighth Schedule as specially designated languages, the Scheduled Languages. Through a series of additions to the list, the number of Scheduled Languages at present is twenty-two.

The years from 1947 to 1956 were quite tumultuous from the language perspective. First, there was a committee set up in 1948 by Dr Rajendra Prasad (1884–1963) to examine if linguistic states would be a viable idea. Then, another committee was set up in the same year that included Jawaharlal Nehru (1889–1964), Vallabhbhai Patel (1875–1950), and Pattabhi Sitaramayya (1880–1959) to examine the proposition. Dr Ambedkar (1891–1956) too, submitted a memorandum asking for a state for Marathi-speakers. Potti Sriramulu (1901–1952), asking for an Andhra Pradesh for Telugu, died in a fast unto death. Finally, a States Reorganization Commission was appointed in 1955, and on its recommendations several states were created with language as the core of the state identity. However, throughout this process the idea of India as a nation with many languages had been firmly accepted by people and, most importantly, was already enshrined in the Constitution. Five years later, when the census for 1961 was conducted, it showed a remarkable degree of confidence in the idea by listing 1,652 mother tongues as being in existence and claimed by the people of India as their mother tongues.

As a result of the extensive debates on the language issue, the Constitution took an extremely nuanced stand. Article

120 provided for the use of Hindi or English for business in the Parliament. Article 210 provided for the use of the state language or Hindi/English for the business of State Assemblies. Article 344 provided for a Language Commission for the upkeep of all languages included in the Eighth Schedule. Article 343 stipulated a fixed period of fifteen years for replacing English with Hindi, but in a sub-clause also provided for further extending the period if such an extension was found necessary; and Article 347 empowered the President to recognize any languages not included in the Eighth Schedule as 'State Languages' if a substantial number of people made such a demand. Thus, while the Constitution laid down the objective of replacing English with Hindi, it also underscored the improbability of doing so within a very short period and also validated the democratic aspiration of various language communities to have their languages included in the Eighth Schedule or, at least, recognized as the 'State Languages' within their own state.

After Independence, by embracing language as the backbone of the state reorganization process, the government of India unmistakably affirmed the concept of a unified nation thriving amidst linguistic diversity. This is not to say that the promotion of Hindi as a possible replacement for English was overlooked. In fact, this goal was frequently emphasized in speeches and supported through grants. A Hindi *kosh* (compendium) for providing terminology was mooted and a yearly Hindi week was made mandatory. It is another matter that the *kosh* soon became a butt of ridicule owing to its preference for Sanskrit-based terminology which was found literally unpalatable and ignored the ease of communication.

Language, like other prominent identity markers, is an emotive issue. No government so far has had the courage to openly accept a complete replacement of the English language by Hindi in the working of Parliament and the administration, in communication between the states and the Centre, in higher education and research, and in industry and business; it is a near impossibility. Besides, the Indian demographics are such that owning up to the reality could be politically suicidal for any party or government. Therefore, successive governments have presented the official language data to show a constant growth of Hindi. In 1971, out of 54.82-crore population, 20.28 crore were reported as Hindi-speaking. In successive census counts, the figures for Hindi were shown as steadily rising: 1981: 25.77 crore out of 66.52 crore, 1991: 32.95 crore out of 83.86 crore, 2001: 42.20 crore out of 102.86 crore; 2011: 52.83 crore out of 121.08 crore. The percentile proportion of Hindi speakers to India's total population was placed at 36.99 per cent (1971), 38.74 per cent (1981), 39.29 per cent (1991), 41.03 per cent (2001), and 43.63 per cent (2011). What the census does not explicitly mention is that since 1971, several 'other' languages have been brought under the rubric of the Hindi language.

The 1,652 mother tongues mentioned in 1961 were reduced to a mere 108 languages in 1971 by introducing a cut-off point of 10,000 for any group of speakers to have their mother tongue listed in the published data. The cut-off point has no scientific basis either in linguistics or statistics.

Its justification is drawn from the politics of electoral democracy. It would be interesting to see the language data of the most recent census which was carried out in 2011. In it, the speakers who claimed Hindi as their mother tongue totalled 32.22 crore. But, in order to bolster the number, the following fifty-three other languages, most of them completely independent as languages and some like Banjari even mutually unintelligible with Hindi, were shown as subsets of Hindi:

Awadhi 3,850,906; Baghati Pahari 15,835; Bagel/Bagel Kandy 2,679,129; Bagri Rajasthan 234,227; Bandar 1,581,271; Bhadrawahi 98,806; Bhagoria 20,924; Bharmauri/Gaddi 181,069; Bhojpuri 50,579,447; Bishnoi 12,079; Brajbhasha 1,556,314; Bundeli/Bundel khandi 5,626,356; Chambeali/Chamrali 125,746; Chhattisgarhi 16,245,190; Churahi 75,552; Dhundhari 1,476,446; Gawari 19,062; Gojri/Gujjari/Gujar 1,227,901; Handuri 47,803; Hara/Harauti 2,944,356; Haryanvi 9,806,519; Jaunpuri/Jaunsari 136,779; Kangri 1,117,342; Khari Boli 50,195; Khortha/Khotta 8,038,735; Kulvi 196,295; Kumauni 2,081,057; Kurmali Thar 311,175; Lamani/Lambadi/Labani 3,276,548; Laria 89,876; Magadhi/Magahi 12,706,825; Malvi 5,212,617; Mandeali 622,590; Marwari 7,831,749; Mewari 4,212,262; Mewati 856,643; Nagpuria 763,014; Nimadi 2,309,265; Padari 17,279; Pahari 3,253,889; Palmuha 23,579; Panch Pargania 244,914; Pando/Pandwani 15,595; Pangwali 18,668; Pawari/Powari 325,772; Puran/Puran Bhasha 12,375; Rajasthani

25,806,344; Sadan/Sadri 4,345,677; Sirmauri 107,401; Sondwari 229,788; Sugali 170,987; Surgujia 1,738,256; and Surjapuri 2,256,228.

If one were to remove these from Hindi, the ratio of the Hindi speakers (32.22 crore) to the total population enumerated by the 2011 census (121.08 crore) would be approximately 1:4. All of this cold data, otherwise fairly uninteresting, goes to show why no government so far has been able to entirely replace either the regional languages or the English language entirely with Hindi.

William Jones's hypothesis initiated a new interest in the prehistory of Sanskrit. Subsequent researches, mostly during the twentieth century, have indicated that there have been at least five major language families in India: (1) Indo-European; (a) Indo-Aryan, (b) Germanic, (2) Dravidian, (3) Austro-Asiatic, (4) Tibet-Burmese, (5) Semito-Hamitic. One may as well include in the list the Andamanese language family and various language isolates. All the languages listed in the Eighth Schedule of the Constitution belong to the first two families, and those that are not listed belong mostly to the remaining language families. Half a century ago, the categorization of Indian languages into families was conducted, yielding the following classification:

I. Indo-European

(a) Indo-Aryan: 1. Assamese(s); 2. Bengali(s); 3. Bhili/Bhilodi; 4. Bishnupuriya; 5. Dogri; 6. Gujarati(s); 7. Halabi; 8. Hindi(s); 9. Kashmiri(s); 10. Khandeshi; 11. Konkani(s); 12. Lahnada; 13. Marathi(s); 14.

Nepali(s); 15. Odia(s); 16. Punjabi(s); 17. Sanskrit(s); 18. Sindhi(s); 19. Urdu(s).

(b) Germanic: 1.English.

II. Dravidian: 1. Coorgi/Kodagu; 2. Gondi; 3. Jatapu; 4. Kannada(s); 5. Khond/Kondh; 6. Kisan; 7. Kolami; 8. Konda; 9. Koya; 10. Kui; 11. Kurukh/Oraon; 12. Malayalam(s); 13. Malto; 14. Parji; 15. Tamil(s); 16. Telugu(s); 17. Tulu.

III. Austro-Asiatic: 1. Bhumij; 2. Gadaba; 3. Ho; 4. Juang; 5. Kharia; 6. Khasi; 7. Koda/Kora; 8. Korku; 9. Korwa; 10. Munda; 11. Mundari; 12. Nicobarese; 13. Santali; 14. Savara.

IV. Tibeto-Burmese: 1. Adi; 2. Anal; 3. Angami; 4. Ao; 5. Bhotia; 6. Bodo/Boro; 7. Chakesang; 8. Chakru/Chokri; 9. Chang; 10. Deori; 11. Dimasa; 12. Gangte; 13. Garo; 14. Halam; 15. Hmar; 16. Kabul; 17. Karbi/Mikir; 18. Khezha; 19. Khiemnungan; 20. Kinnauri; 21. Koch; 22. Kom; 23. Konyak; 24. Kuki; 25. Lahuli; 26.Lakher; 27. Lalung; 28. Lepcha; 29. Liangmei; 30. Limbu; 31. Lotha; 32. Lushai/Mizo; 33. Manipuri(s); 34. Mao; 35. Maram; 36. Maring; 37. Miri/Mishing; 38. Mishmi; 39. Mogh; 40. Monpa; 41. Nissi/Dafla; 42. Nocte; 43. Paite; 44. Pawl; 45. Phom; 46. Pochury; 47. Rabha; 48. Rengma; 49. Sangtam; 50. Sema; 51. Sherpa; 52. Tangkhul; 53. Tangsa; 54. Thado; 55. Tibetan; 56. Tripuri; 57. Vaiphei; 58. Wancho; 59. Yimchunger; 60. Zeliang; 61. Zemi; 62. Zou.

V. Semito-Haematic: 1. Arabic/Arbi.

More recent classification, as proposed by the linguist Anvita Abbi (*Histories of a Civilisation*, p. 238) is as follows:

i. Indo-Aryan (Northern parts of India)
ii. Dravidian (Southern parts of India)
iii. Austroasiatic: a) Mon-Khmer (Northeast), Nico-Monic (the Nicobar Islands), Munda (Central and Eastern India)
iv. Tibeto-Burman (Himalayan Ranges)
v Tai-Kadai (Assam and Arunachal Pradesh)
vi Great Andamanese (The Andaman Island)
vii Indian Sign Languages (spread across the country)
viii. Isolates: a) Shom Pen (the Nicobar Islands), b) Nihali/Nahali (Maharashtra), c) Angan (Andaman Islands)

MULTILINGUAL CULTURE

Among the many essential features of a given culture, whether they are material or intangible, language is without doubt the most crucial. In fact, it would be nearly impossible to think of culture in the absence of the sign systems that we call language, both, because thought is primarily semantic and because cultural systems approximate very closely to the linguistic systems through which they circulate in manifest forms. Over the last two decades, scientists have come up with mathematical models for predicting the life of languages (Braggs and Freedman, 1993). These predictions have invariably indicated that the human species is moving rapidly towards the extinction of a large part of its linguistic heritage. The predictions do not agree on the exact magnitude of the impending disaster; but they all agree on the fact that close to three quarters or more of all existing natural human languages are in a state of decline and on the verge of extinction. There are, on the other hand, advocates of linguistic globalisation. The processes of globalisation have found it necessary to promote homogenized cultures. The idea has found support among the classes that stand to benefit by the globalisation of economies. They would prefer the spread of one or only a few languages all over the world so that communication across national boundaries becomes incredibly easy. Obviously, the nations and communities that have learnt to live within a single language, whose economic well-being is not dependent on knowing languages other than their own, whose knowledge systems are firmly safeguarded within their own languages, will not experience the stress of language-loss—at least not immediately. The loss of the world's total language heritage, which will weaken the global stock of human intellect and civilizations, will have numerous indirect enfeebling effects on them too. Since it is primarily language that makes us human and distinguishes us from other species and animate nature (Blench, 2012), and since the human consciousness specifically functions given the ability for linguistic expression, it becomes necessary to recognize language as the most crucial aspect of the cultural capital.

It has taken human beings continuous work of about half a million years to accumulate this valuable capital (Corballis, 2011). In our time we have come close to the point of losing most of it. Historians of civilization tell us that probably a comparable, though not exactly similar, situation had arisen in the past some seven or eight thousand years ago (Crystal, 2000). This was when human beings discovered the magic of nature that seeds are. When the shift from an entirely hunting-gathering or pastoralist economies to early agrarian economies started taking place, we are told, the language diversity of the world was severely affected (Blench and Spriggs, 2012, Corballis, 2011). It may not be wrong to surmise that the current crisis in human languages, too, is triggered by the fundamental economic shift that has enveloped the entire world—in the North or South, East or West. This time, though, the crisis has an added theme as a lot of the human activity is dominated by man-made intelligence.

The technologies aligned with artificial intelligence have all been depending heavily on modelling the activity of the human mind along the linguistic transactions. The intelligent machines modelled after entirely neurological or psychological systems are still not commonly in use. The language-based technologies are now well-entrenched partners in the semantic universe(s) that bind various communities together (Gillespie, 2007). Therefore, that universe is being reshaped. Language today is as much a system of meaning in the cyberspace effecting communication between a machine and another machine as it has been a system of meaning in the social space achieving communication between a human being and another human being. Neurologists explain the current shift in man's cognitive processes by pointing to the rapidly changing ways in which the brain stores and analyses sensory perceptions as well as information. Linguists have raised an alarm about the sinking fortunes of natural languages through which human communication has taken place over the last seventy millennia. They have started noticing that the use of man-made memory chips in intelligent machines causes decline in the human ability to remember. The impact is felt by tense structures of many natural languages, particularly the past-tense structure. Technologists, particularly those astride the leading glory of technology—the ICT—have been talking of network communities as a substitute for civilizations. All in all, there is excitement in the air, and there is alarm in the minds. This is so on all fronts of knowledge, in all aspects of social organizations and all branches of human experience. Collectively, for all nations, all ethnic and cultural groups of humans, the vision of a life well beyond our imagination has started appearing on the horizon even if it has not become fully manifest, making a mockery of all that the human brain and mind have so far held as being natural and permanent.

In the new experience of the world waiting for all of us, memory as we have so far used it (Rossi, 2006) is expected to be of little use, and imagination as we have so far exercised it is predicted to get entirely transformed. *Homo sapiens*, it is believed, moving out of memory, imagination and even language, are poised to enter a post-human phase of the natural evolution (McMohan and McMohan, 2013). Man and the intelligent machine, together, are expected to develop a new image-based system of communication, a new post-human and predominantly externalized memory, and a sphere of imagination where multiple frames of existence seamlessly collide. The short-term future implications for the global language crisis for African and Asian countries will be, first and foremost, an increased migration of the economically less privileged classes from one geographical area to another, a marked change in the perception of identity, a more deep-cutting social segregation, and most regrettably, the alienation of the traditional knowledge, ecological as well as sociological. The social, cultural and economic imbalances created by these projected conditions can well be imagined. And that kind of imagined future is already an important part of the activist rhetoric in vogue (because of its international presence) at present. However, what is not yet imagined is that the massive language migration may offer many of these countries an opportunity to reconceive the urban habitat. This point calls for some elaboration.

When the state organization was carried out in India during the two decades after independence and linguistic states were proposed, the assumption was that language would help in keeping the people of a linguistically conceptualized state emotionally bound together (Schwartzberg, 2009 and Sarangi, 2009). For reasons that had roots in the idea that *matri-bhumi* (motherland) and *matri-bhasha* (mother tongue) are closely analogous, such a state was seen as a 'homogenous' state. However, owing to the economic and demographic histories of the capital cities of many of the states, a typical megacity has emerged as being at a fundamental variance from the rest of the state. Thus, the linguistic composition of Mumbai is not at all like the linguistic composition of the rest of Maharashtra. The same is the case with Bangalore, Hyderabad, Kolkata, Chandigarh and Ahmedabad. Yet, the school boards and the textbook boards in the states continue to look at the megapolis and the rest of the state as being one or alike. The language decisions of governments and educational regulatory bodies have ceased to be realistic and appropriate. When, in the near future, the larger cities start recognizing their essentially multilingual character, despite their being capitals of a given linguistic state, a more congenial atmosphere shall emerge for preservation and perpetuation of diverse languages. Capital cities of most of the states would have to be delinked from the states in some ways and probably they will have to be given the status of union territories. The delinking will not be called for merely because of the linguistic composition of the megacities, as language remains far low in the hierarchy of priorities of any overpopulated country. Yet, the economic realities such as the cost-benefit ratio and revenue efficiency, energy consumption and production abilities, global market space and global skilled labour available in the key urban centres, will push the public opinion in the direction of a relatively greater autonomy for such cities.

By 2047, a century from the date of India's independence, cities like Delhi, Mumbai, Hyderabad, and Bengaluru are likely to have the strong presence of about ten international languages—English (also American English), Korean, Chinese, Arabic, French, Spanish, German, Russian, Italian, Japanese—over thirty Scheduled Languages, eight to ten Asian languages, and a hundred or more minor and tribal languages. Thus, these cities will be home to nearly 150 or more languages, each of these with their individual 'network communities'—wired and economically productive. Entirely out of economic realism and political pragmatism, the big Indian cities will learn to acknowledge the 'multilingual' nature of their demographic composition and make moves in the direction of establishing multilingual schools, knowledge parks, libraries, book malls, TV channels, radio broadcast, etc. The cities in all probability will play out the 'multicultural phase' of development that European nations studded with migrant labourers have gone through in the recent past (Bianco, 2012). But, given the Indian adherence to 'traditionalism', our lasting love for the past and memory that glorifies the past, and the reinforcement of the sense of identity bruised by the big cities, the rest of the state/s comprising small towns and deserted villages, tourist resorts and temple towns, may return to be focal points in linguistic chauviṇism and cultural jingoism. In this imagined future, probably, the nation may appear to assuage itself for a while of the mournful awareness that humans have started departing from natural languages a bit too rapidly (Cru, 2010). Yet, in the process, perhaps, India will learn to respect what has always been an essential feature of Indian society for the last five millennia, namely, that a single language as a mother tongue is but an abstract notion without any substantial evidence in the social reality. We may wake up to the realization that India has always nurtured and worshipped languages, welcomed languages from foreign lands, and tamed even the mightiest of languages (such as Sanskrit and Persian) in the interest of the voices of the small communities. We may wake up to this realization when natural language itself will face a threat to its continuation as never before.

One needs to address a common misgiving that seems to have pervaded the popular sentiment. It relates to the place of the English language. Ever since the English language was introduced in the higher education in India as the main language of knowledge, a slow process flagged off by Lord T. B. Macaulay's 'Minutes' (1835), there have been undercurrents within Indian languages that have viewed English as a challenge (Mayhew, 1926). In the years immediately following Independence, there have been protest movements in the South against Hindi and an active anti-English campaign in the Northern parts of the country. As a result of the exponential growth in the number of English medium schools in the country in recent years, one notices the eruption of *bhasha-bachao* (save our language) movements in several states, most particularly in Maharashtra, Gujarat, Karnataka, and Punjab. It is easy to understand that the anti-English protests and campaigns shape up as the English language has played several key roles in the history of India since the eighteenth century, apart from being just a natural language that came here like many such languages. It has been the language of the people who had colonized India. It has been the language through which a lot of what we call 'modernity' is supposed to have reached the Indian shores. It has been the language of the twentieth century imperialism which the political sentiment in India did not favour so much. Besides, English is today the language of a powerful communication technology, and the language associated with the flow of international capital. Being thus so many of the above, and more, it continues to elicit anger from a variety of quarters from time to time.

Yet, it is a language that has brought to Indian languages a very huge range of lexical items adding to their power of expression. It is the language which has continued to enrich the literary and dramatic expression in Indian languages by bringing to them literature from all parts of the world. Besides, it is today probably the most effective link language for the Indian republic and a language which brings employment and business more easily than other languages do. Given this extremely complicated and entrenched place of the English language in India, what is in store for us in the near future? More specifically, what will be the condition of the Indian languages such as Bangla, Telugu, Marathi, and Gujarati and so on? Will English manage to replace all of them completely? Or, will English one day beat a quiet retreat to the lonely island from where it came? It is but natural that these and such other questions should continue to exercise the minds of the nation-loving Indians.

Obviously, there are no easy answers to these questions since human languages are known to have behaved in the most surprising manner in the past. Some very mighty languages are known to have disappeared in the face of some minor challenges; some others have grown taller precisely because they faced threats of extinction. Yet, if one were to try predicting the fortunes of the English language in India, one would have to look at the history of its fortunes in similar situations elsewhere. It is necessary to recall that the English language travelled with the colonial rulers to several other continents. It managed to almost entirely replace the indigenous languages in North America, Australia, and New Zealand. That did not, however, happen in African countries like Nigeria, Kenya, and South Africa. In India, just as the fortunes of the English language continued to improve, numerous Indian languages too witnessed a remarkable literary and linguistic growth in the same period. Based on this comparative perspective, one can perhaps propose that there had been something in the making of the Indian languages prior to the arrival of English which allowed them to face the encounter in a far more mature way than the languages of the Atlantic and Pacific areas had managed to do. What was this peculiar strength?

If one were to step back in history, one notices that the Indic and the Dravidic languages had previously negotiated the encounter with Arabic and Persian with an equal maturity, themselves surviving in the encounter and linguistically gaining in the process. Given such a history, it is reasonable to assume that the innate multilingualism of the colonized culture(s) will see them through in the current encounter with the English language. As a result of the intimacy between English and the indigenous languages, they are likely to get suffused with English vocabulary. But so long as the grammars are their own, they need not fear a total annihilation at the hands of English.

The fear of decline should arise from another quarter, namely, the neglect of the minor languages, the dialects, and the speech patterns of the indigenous communities, the forest dwellers, the hill communities and the coastal communities. These 'other' languages have been like the roots of the main languages in Asia and Africa. In the past, they have provided the main languages semantic resource and expressive power. Those roots have started drying up as the speakers of the 'other'—the non-recognized, the oral, the economically less privileged—languages are driven to outward migration in search of livelihood. Already the erosion of the supporting indigenous languages has started showing an adverse impact on the main languages of Africa and Asia. The situation would be predictably far worse some thirty years from now. So, if the great language diversity of the world has to be preserved, promoted and carried forward to the future generations, it would be necessary to turn attention to the indigenous and minor languages.

Language is not only a social system of verbal icons, arbitrarily assembled through ages, it is also a 'means' of carrying forward the cumulative human experience of millennia to the future generations. When language trajectories are snapped, the accumulated wisdom in those languages too gets submerged and continues to survive in severely truncated, irreparable, and insensible forms. Therefore, only if a perceptible shift takes place in our attitude to what knowledge is, how it is transmitted to new generations and how it is harnessed for improving sustainability of the planet earth, can the continuation of some of the languages be ensured. That shall also contribute significantly to the deepening of democracies in a people-friendly and ecology-friendly form.

In human history, language was created as a 'surplus' of man's cognitive and emotive transactions, a product of the 'labour of the mind'. For a very long span of the human history, language continued to retain its character as a predominantly 'free' system that is sturdily resistant to government controls, market regulations and cultural oppressions.

However, over the last few centuries, particularly since the rise of technologies that function to assist language transactions—printing, photography, electronic-language-storage-and-reproduction, digital-encoding-and-decoding of human language—language acquisition, language transmission, and language use have started getting rapidly monetized. Today, as never before, the economically disposed classes all over the world are finding it difficult to access language acquisition as per their needs and desires. Thus, throughout the world, we now notice a digit-powered linguistic class and another print and digit deprived linguistic class. The divide is too deep to bridge by following any conventional or prevailing economic ideologies. A technological reversal in the evolution of languages too is a hugely unrealistic proposition. The only hope for ensuring any future for the linguistic *Homo sapiens* is to envision together and integrate economic development and linguistic federalism. If the rural landscapes and marginalized communities can be safeguarded, the currently threatened languages will find a safe passage to the future; and only if those languages continue to survive shall we have access to the knowledge that helps us build a sustainable future society. The two are so intricately linked.

LANGUAGES AND THE STATE

One of the most significant features of Indian civilization is its immense linguistic variety. Given that languages show marked variations in their phonological behaviour from one geographical region to another, it is but natural that a vast geographical expanse such as India should give rise to a large variety of dialects. But not all large countries have such a variety as India has. This is so mainly because of India's peculiar history of assimilation of different cultures during the course of the last three millennia. The result is that, with its wealth of more than twenty written languages and over seven hundred other languages, India is today a unique 'linguistic area'.

For any nation-state in the world, it becomes necessary to regulate the growth and development of languages in order to keep the country together and at the same time to do proper justice to the nature and identity of its linguistic heritage. This problem had been a part of the deliberations that contributed to the drafting of India's Constitution, which provides the foundation for various policies for cultural development in independent India. During the pre-Independence era, debates arose concerning which language should be designated as the national language, which one should serve as the language of administration, and how many languages could accommodate literary programmes. As a result, the makers of our Constitution decided to include a special schedule of languages. Hindi, included in the Schedule of Languages, was expected to be elevated to the status of the national language, but provision was also made for English to perform that function for a limited period of ten years. Thirteen other languages were included as the languages of administration. The reason for not including yet more languages was that it would be impractical to run the business of the government and the judiciary in each and every language. Subsequently, through Constitutional amendments, more languages were added to the Eighth Schedule. The other statutory bodies, which had to deal with languages and literature, followed, more or less, the principles laid down in the Constitution; but they added to this list a few more as and when the need was felt. Thus, the Sahitya Akademi and the National Book Trust have been publishing books in twenty-two languages.

The Census of India 2011 data related to languages was released by the census office in 2018. With all its tables and charts, it looks perfectly harmless. But, scratch the surface and you find that it is heavily doctored. It tells us that in 2011, our countrymen stated a total of 19,569 'raw returns' (read, non-doctored claims). Out of these, close to 17,000 were outright rejected, and another 1,474 were dumped because not enough scholarly corroboration for them exists. Only 1,369, roughly 6 per cent of the total claims, were admitted as 'classified mother tongues'. Rather than placing them as languages, they were grouped under 121 headings. These 121 were declared as languages of India. One may ask, but how does this matter? It matters because the data for Hindi has been bolstered up—shown at 52 plus crore—by adding to its core figure of speakers, the speakers of nearly fifty other languages. These include Bhojpuri, claimed by over five crore, many languages in Rajasthan, Himachal Pradesh,

Uttarakhand, Haryana, and Bihar, claimed by close to a total six crore. At the same time seventeen of the twenty-two Scheduled Languages are reported by the census as showing a downward trend in their rate of growth in comparison to the growth in the previous decade. The architecture of the presentation of the language census data has at its foundation the principle of exclusion. And the exclusion is imposed on the languages that people of India have claimed in the census exercise as being their languages. To use a term from medical sciences, this act amounts to imposing an involuntary aphasia on citizens. In this instance, the numbers on whom it is imposed run into crores. And that is no small matter.

Over the last eighty years, successive governments have carried out a decadal census. The 1931 census was quite a landmark as it held a clear mirror before the country about the caste and community composition. The next year was exceptional as the war disrupted the exercise. Again, 1951 was a rather busy year for the new Indian republic. It was during the 1961 census that languages in the country were enumerated fully. India learnt through it that a total of 1,652 mother tongues were being spoken. Through a rather ill-founded logic, this figure was pegged in the 1971 census at only 109, a reduction of 1,543. 'The logic was a language deserving respectability should not have less than 10,000 speakers. On no scientific grounds a fair decision; but it has stuck and the practice continues to be followed' (Devy, 2014).

The language enumeration takes place in the first year of every decade. The data collected is disclosed to the public some six or seven years later. This is so as the processing of language data is far more time consuming than processing economic or other scientific data. In 2018, the Census of India declared the language data of the 2011 census. The scale of the entire exercise is simply unprecedented. It takes into account 1.20 billion speakers of a very large number of languages. The Language division of the census office therefore deserves applause. Yet, the data presented leaves one with more questions than before.

During the census, the citizens of India provided 19,569 names of mother tongues. In technical terms these are called 'raw returns'. Based on previously available linguistic and sociological information, the authorities decided that of these, 18,200 did not match 'logically' with known information. A total of 1,369 names ('labels' as they are technically called) were picked up as 'being names of languages'. The 'raw returns' left out represent nearly six million citizens. Thanks to the classification regime, their linguistic citizenship is just axed. Then, in addition to the 1,369 'mother tongue' names shortlisted in scrutiny, there were 1,474 other mother tongue names. They were placed under the generic label 'Others'. These linguistic others are not seen as any concern of the census! They have languages of their own. They speak, but the classification system could not identify what or which languages they speak. They are simply silenced by slapping an apparently innocuous label on them. Others!

The fortunate 1,369 were further grouped together under a total of 121 'group labels'. These are presented to the country as 'Languages'. Of these twenty-two are the languages included in the Eighth Schedule of the

Constitution. So, they are called the 'scheduled' languages. The remaining ninety-nine are described as the 'non-scheduled' languages. When one starts looking at these, one finds that most of the groupings are forced. For instance, under the heading 'Hindi', there are nearly fifty other languages. Bhojpuri spoken by more than fifty million, with its own cinema, theatre, literature, vocabulary and style, is listed as 'Hindi'. Nearly thirty million of the population from Rajasthan with its own independent languages too is listed as speaking Hindi as the mother tongue. The Powari/Pawri of the tribal in Maharashtra and Madhya Pradesh has been hitched to it. So, too, is the Kumauni of Uttarakhand yoked to Hindi. The report states that 528,347,193 speak Hindi as their mother tongue. And this simply is not so. One expects that the census should in the minimum adequately reflect the linguistic composition of the country. Giving cold figures that help neither educators nor policymakers, and not least the speakers of languages themselves, is a practice that deserves to be brought to an end.

Since our Constitution gives us the fundamental and non-negotiable right to free expression, and since it not only accepts but encourages the idea of a multilingual India, is there not something profoundly unconstitutional in intimidating writers and thinkers, or in wilfully suppressing people's languages? The UNESCO brief for language rights describes denial of mother tongues or any wilful concealment of mother tongue by the member states as equivalent to genocide. A strong word, indeed, but, necessary, thinks UNESCO. Quite ironically, the justification for both these actions is drawn from a common source—a deeply flawed idea of nationalism. It holds that anyone critical of the current regime is an enemy of India, an anti-national trying to 'spread disaffection towards the state'; in simpler words, seditious. With respect to languages, the argument says that if we have any large multiplicity of languages, it may result in the disintegration of our national territory. The love for the nation and its integrity are of course of prime importance. But a nation becomes great by the thought and knowledge it produces, by nurturing the freedom of mind and by the fearlessness of its citizens. States that consciously encourage creating societies incapable of critiquing the system generate what the ancient Latin described as hegemony. And, governments that become intolerant of difference of opinion become heavy with hubris. Hubris and hegemony produce a pervasive mediocrity. Excessively proud rulers, intellectual mediocrity, and lynching mobs form a combine that threatens speech and forces civilizations to shut their minds.

It was a remarkable foresight of the makers of the Indian Constitution to create a dedicated Schedule of Languages—the Eighth Schedule—which initially included fourteen languages as the languages of administration. This was a radical departure from the European idea of nationalism based on linguistic uniformity. The list in the Schedule was subsequently enlarged so as to adjust the intent of the Schedule to the linguistic realities in the country. The languages, popularly known as the 'Scheduled Languages', are Assamiya, Bangla, Boro, Dogri, Gujarati, Hindi, Kannada, Kashmiri, Konkani, Maithili, Malayalam, Manipuri, Marathi,

Nepali, Odia, Punjabi, Sanskrit, Santali, Sindhi, Tamil, Telugu and Urdu. The Constitution empowers individual states to identify any language/s as official language/s even if it is not in the Eighth Schedule. Thus, though not in the Schedule, Kokborok (Tripura), Khasi and Garo (Meghalaya), and Mizo (Mizoram) enjoy the status of 'official' languages of administration. Further, a state has the powers to offer primary school education in any language irrespective of its official status. Under this provision, a number of languages of Adivasi communities have been introduced in primary schools in Orissa, Chhattisgarh, Andhra Pradesh, Maharashtra, and Gujarat where the population speaking those languages is significant. In some states, new link-languages are conceptualized and promoted in order to keep the linguistically diverse states together. Rajasthani (Rajasthan), Pahari (Himachal Pradesh), and Nagamese (Nagaland) are the instances of such state-promoted 'binding' languages.

During the last hundred years, the print-culture has reached a number of languages that are not officially recognized or promoted. Though it is not widely known, the number of little magazines, pamphlets and small-circulation books produced in the Non-Scheduled Languages is quite large, a phenomenon that led the National Book Trust (NBT) to make tribal language publications the central theme for the NBT's International Book Fair in 2014. The All India Radio (AIR) operates in twenty-seven Indian and foreign languages and offers weekly slots to nearly thirty tribal or sub-regional languages in its regional programmes. In addition to the languages mentioned so far, there are numerous other major languages in India. Some are native such as Kutchhi (Gujarat), Tulu (Karnataka), Bhojpuri (UP, Bihar) and Bagadi (Rajasthan), while others have come from other countries and cultures and were accepted in the course of history as 'our languages'. The 'foreign' languages which are still in use in different parts of the country primarily include English. However, in small pockets, French, Portuguese, Bhoti, Iranian, Arabic, Persian, Karen, and Pashto are spoken.

During its history of several millennia, the Indian subcontinent accepted language legacies as distinct as the Avestan of the Zoarastrians, the Austro-Asiatic of the Pacific, the Tibeto-Burman of the East and Northeast Asia. The Indic (or the Indo-Aryan) languages in the Northern states together with the Dravidic languages in the South and the Tibeto-Burman languages in the Northeast, each with a great variety of sub-branches make for the larger bulk of the Indian languages. Throughout the known history of the subcontinent, there has been an active exchange and cultural osmosis between the indigenous languages and the migratory languages, producing in the process great literature in many of them. Numerically speaking, India is home to one out of every eight languages on earth. The diversity is impressive not only in numerical terms. A language is not just a communication system, it is also a unique world-view. Thus, though one can translate a given meaning from one language to another, there are always shades of meaning and nuances in any language that simply cannot be translated into other languages. Hence, the great diversity of languages in India needs to be seen as the diversity of world-views, of the unique ways of perceiving the world.

Despite the existing linguistic diversity in India, the language stock in the country has started showing signs of a rapid decline. Several historical factors appear to be responsible for the decline. The print technology impacted Indian languages profoundly during the nineteenth century. The languages that were printed acquired importance, the ones that remained untouched by it came to be seen more as dialects than as languages. The reorganization of Indian states mainly as linguistic states turned the already marginalized and 'non-printed' languages into 'minority' languages. Thus, Bhili, a major language in itself with over two crore speakers, got divided into four states and became a minority language in all of them—Maharashtra, Madhya Pradesh, Gujarat, and Rajasthan.

The list of 'Mother Tongues' reported by the 1961 census had 1,652 names. Beginning with the 1971 census, the government decided to include in the list only the languages which had more than 10,000 speakers. The list of 1971 had a total of 108 names, with an additional entry (109)—of 'all others'. The policy of using a cut-off figure further eliminated the already marginalized and minor languages. They started becoming increasingly invisible in social practice or political discourse. The relative lack of livelihood possibilities in the areas where the minor and marginalized languages are spoken has led to an exodus to areas where major and mainstream languages are spoken. Thus, the language diversity that people have nurtured over millennia, and which the Constitution has guaranteed, is under attack due to the state's attitude to it. The number of languages that may have disappeared since 1961 is estimated to be 250, eliminating in the process nearly a quarter of India's 'world-views'.

The 'imposition' of Hindi insidiously planted in the New Education Policy may appear at first sight desirable to any pseudo-nationalist; but it will cause irreversible harm to our language diversity. 'Nation' is not only an emotive idea; it implies 'people' and 'their cultural traditions'. Language is the very basis of community and its tradition. Let us hope that language democracy is not destroyed by pseudo-nationalistic majoritarianism.

A guarantee for providing patronage was enshrined in the Constitution, Article 347, which reads:

> On a demand made in that behalf, the President may, if he is satisfied that a substantial proportion of the population of the State desire the use of any language spoken by them to be recognized by that State, direct that such language shall also be officially recognized throughout that State or any part thereof for such purposes as he may specify.

Thus, language loss, linguistic shifts, and decline in the linguistic heritage cannot be blamed on the structural factors alone. There appear to be other and more overwhelming factors at work, and that is the development discourse in a rapidly globalizing world. One notices now in India, and in other Asian and African countries, an overpowering desire among parents to educate their children through the medium of English, French, or Spanish in the hope that these languages will provide a certain visibility to the children when they grow up in the international market of productive labour. This desire has affected the schooling pattern in favour of an education through an international language not witnessed in any previous era.

The argument in favour of providing children mother tongue education, at least at the primary school level, for a healthy development of their intellect is indeed an incontrovertible one. However, the contrary argument which holds that children not educated in their mother tongues do not achieve a full intellectual development deserves to be reconsidered. If literature is considered to contain the most complex usage of language, one would assume that children who do not get education in their own language will not be capable of fully appreciating, let alone producing, literature in the given language. Historical evidence however shows that such an assumption is not well-founded. Some of the greatest among the world's writers are known to have not received schooling in the languages that they used for creative linguistic production. Shakespeare did his schooling in Latin, so did Milton. Dante was not educated in Italian. Valmiki (date uncertain, prior to the first century BCE) and Kalidasa (fourth/fifth century)—with somewhat hazy histories—did not receive education in Sanskrit. It is not clearly known if Jean Genet had any French schooling, or if William Butler Yeats (1865–1939) had any Gaelic schooling. Geoffrey Chaucer's generation (fourteenth century) of English children had to study French, not English; and in fact, English as a subject was not introduced in schools in England till the Chartist Movement brought up the issue of educating children belonging to the labour classes.

During the early years of the nineteenth century, an interesting debate occupied the centre stage of the social reform movement in India, in which the Bengali intellectuals kept asking for education through the English language medium, while an English officer like Mountstuart Elphinstone (1779–1859) held that the schools in Indian languages would be desirable. The argument came to an end when in 1835; Lord Macaulay's *Minutes on Education* recommended that English would be the medium of all serious education in India. Quite remarkably, it was since then that literatures in modern Indian languages showed a significant creativity. These arguments are not intended to take away any substance from the view that mother tongue education is the most suitable for young learners. I am only pointing to the fact that a lack of access to the mother tongue education is not enough of a cultural condition to destroy human creativity. The more significant condition is of having no hope of survival of a community.

In India, universal education is the obligation of parents and the right of the child. State-sponsored schooling is almost free and clearly affordable for the most deprived. There is provision of mid-day meals for children so that food insecurity does not drive children away from the classrooms. The federal government and the state governments treat school education as one of their primary responsibilities. Child labour is officially made illegal, and even higher education is made free for women in many states. There are provisions for educational reservations for the children belonging to Scheduled Castes and Scheduled Tribes as also for children from Other Backward Communities. The Indian state operates primary schools in nearly fifty Indian languages and several foreign languages. Adult literacy and non-formal schooling are continuously promoted. There are Constitutional guarantees built in the educational programmes aimed at promoting all listed languages. The Central Institute of Indian Languages is charged with the production of educational materials in the marginalized and minority languages.

In spite of such efforts, many marginalized languages and indeed some of the 'major' languages seem to display an inscrutable indifference towards their upkeep. An unimaginably large number of children seem to join schools that charge exorbitant fees and use the English language as the medium of instruction. In sum, the schooling is all geared towards enabling children to join the ever-growing number of institutions of higher learning, more than 70 per cent of which are devoted to Information Technology. When a child joins a school that gives instruction in an Indian language, the act comes to be seen as the beginning of a social disadvantage. Under these circumstances, the preservation of languages, particularly those requiring exceedingly diligent preservation efforts, is quite a daunting task, and not one that can be accomplished merely by initiating structural changes.

The unprecedented situation arising out of the corona virus pandemic may appear to have marked a complete break from the past, a kind of a threshold marking a new epoch. However, one very important strand of continuity between the pre-corona virus and the corona times is the question of diminishing citizenship rights, a kind of a tragic finale of a two-century-old struggle for freedom. The Citizenship Amendment Act (CAA) was passed by the Parliament in the second week of December 2019. Well until the announcement of the lockdown in the third week of March 2020, massive agitations against the CAA, the National Register of Citizens (NRC), and the National Population Register (NPR) rocked the country. During those four months, activists, analysts, and media commented on every aspect of the clash between the current regime's idea of nationalism and the idea of citizenship inscribed in the Constitution. There is one aspect of the question though that did not find much articulation during the agitation. It was related to the position of the minor ethnic-linguistic-religious groups. That apparently insignificant strand had a relatively minor significance during the Citizenship Amendment Act (CAA) debate. But in the post-corona virus epoch, it is likely to acquire greater significance. When the amended Citizenship Act declared that migrants from Bangladesh, Pakistan, and Afghanistan would be given citizenship if they were minorities such as Hindus, Christians, Sikhs, Buddhists, Jains, and Parsis in those countries, the new law left out other minorities who belonged to none of these religions or to the broad spectrum of Islam (such as Shia or Ahmedia). These were Mro, Meitei, Tripura, Marma, Tanchangya, Barua, Khasi, Santhals, Chakma, Garo, Oraons, Mundas, Marmas, Tripperas, and Tanchangya, all listed in Bangladesh as minorities. What marks out all these communities is that apart from being theologically different, they are primarily linguistic communities. Each of them speaks a distinct language, and the names of their languages and the community names are identical. These are smaller in number in Bangladesh than the other minorities that the CAA had declared as 'welcome' communities, but all of them face multiple vulnerabilities. Besides, all of these have been known in all historical periods to have migrated between what is now Bangladesh and India. Why they were left out should remain an enigma till we turn our attention to the regime's handling of another aspect of the citizenship-language issue.

Since Independence, Indians have accepted language diversity as a social norm and an inalienable feature of the Indian nation. India's Constitution endorses language diversity at least as a 'noble intention' if not as a non-negotiable right of the republic. As citizens, we waste no opportunity to state our tolerance towards different languages. When nationalism emerged in Europe during the nineteenth century, conformity to a 'national language' was seen as an attribute of citizenship. Though inspired by Europe's ideas of nationalism, the Indian struggle for independence did not get bogged down by any linguistic chauvinism. In social and personal spaces, formal and informal, numerous languages have continued to coexist in India in the ancient and medieval past and during the seven decades since Independence. Yet, there are some grey areas in India's knowledge about its linguistic diversity: the country does not know how many languages its people really speak; there is still a mix of myth and history surrounding their emergence and evolution.

In ancient and medieval sources, there is an impressive range of writings on the etymology, grammar, semantics, and philosophy of language. In works by scholars such as Panini (fourth century BCE), Matanga (sixth century CE), Dandin (seventh century CE), Rajasekhara (tenth century CE), Al-Biruni (970–1048) and Amir Khusrow (1253–1325) we get details of various languages spoken in the Indian subcontinent. However, no exact inventory of all the languages was ever available. The first such enumeration was by Grierson, who worked in the colonial administration. He toiled for a good three decades to prepare the first and fairly definitive survey, and in the first two decades of the twentieth century produced eleven volumes in nineteen parts that offered a good descriptive record of 189 languages and several hundred of what he classified as 'dialects'. His description was based on the edifice of modern linguistics which, in turn, was quickened a century before him by William Jones's chance observation about the striking similarity between the stock of words in Greek, Latin, Sanskrit, and Persian. The map of India has changed since Grierson's time. After Independence, Indian authorities should have carried out a fresh survey. That exercise, however, remained desired but never accomplished until a group of volunteers decided to make an attempt and compiled the *People's Linguistic Survey of India* (2010-13). Invariably, in the absence of a definitive Survey of Language for all its language data requirements, the country depended more on the census count of languages.

The census, conducted every decade, which was scheduled to be carried out in 2021, has not taken place.

One can imagine the outcome of the next language count going by what was released in June 2018 as the 'Language Data of 2011 Census'. The census had a question about the mother tongue. It had another question about 'languages known other than the mother tongue'. All responses to this question indicating Sanskrit as one of the 'other languages' were counted as if this was the answer to the first language. Therefore, when we total the number of speakers of all mother tongues (and the mother tongues not counted in the final record), and remove the people who use sign language (and do not speak any other language) the figure we get is slightly higher than the population of India. The same benefit is not given to English which figures in the response to the second question. A similarly inflated figure was given for Sanskrit by counting the returns given against the question about the 'second language'. As against this, the use of English was not seen through the prism of a second language. Counting of English was restricted to the 'mother tongue' category, in effect, bringing down the number of people speaking English. Considering the widespread use of English in education, law, administration, media and healthcare, a very significant number of Indians use English as a utility language. But the 2011 language census recorded that a total of only 2,59,678 Indians speak English as their 'mother tongue'. Numerically accurate, sociologically disastrous! Regardless of whether the Constitution recognizes the right to expression as a fundamental right, regardless of language being the main means of expression for humans, hundreds of languages of the Adivasis and nomadic communities in India face imminent risk of being wiped out from official records in the service of the Hindu-Hindi nationalism.

In the nineteenth century, when nationalism emerged as a transformative movement in the history of Europe, there were some nations which insisted on a monolingual nation. Some other nations were against such an approach. At the end of the nineteenth century and the first half of the twentieth century, this was the dilemma faced by European and North American people. In Germany and Italy, they opted for a unilingual nation. We all know what happened to both these countries in the twentieth century. Because of their excessively myopic ideas of nationalism, fascism emerged in both the countries. There were other nations, like the US, which did not conceptualize the nation in terms of a single language. Ireland, though fighting for the dignity of the Gaelic, did not rule out the place of the English language in their national life.

We also accepted the ideas of liberty from France, the concept of Sinn Fein movement from Ireland, the philosophy of R. W. Emerson, and the principles—Liberty, Equality, and Fraternity—proposed by the French Revolution, as part of our Independence struggle. As a result, when India was looking at becoming a nation, the leaders realized that we could not possibly be a nation with a single language, a single religion, or a single ethnic group. They were aware that India has been home to numerous people who settled here in various historical periods and have been assimilated into Indian society. They also understood that India had many languages and it was necessary to include, promote, and respect all those languages. Essentially, India's idea of an 'Independent Nation' was that of a multilingual one. The Constitution itself defines India as 'a Union of States'. These States have been primarily carved out as linguistic states.

During the formative years of independent India, almost every meeting of the Constituent Assembly had a discussion on the language question. Since the discussion on the language question could not be concluded, the Assembly, in its wisdom, decided to prepare a list of the most-spoken languages, which then became the Eighth Schedule of the Constitution. There are many other languages which deserve to be included in the Eighth Schedule. The twenty-two languages in the Eighth Schedule have a Constitutional guarantee for their existence and dignity. Despite all this, Hindi is being presented as the official national language. When the Constitution of India was adopted, it was said that English would continue along with Hindi as a language of administration for ten years and Hindi would supplant and replace it later. Since that did not happen, an extension was given. Even then, Hindi was not sufficiently competent to replace English in the national life. In 1974, a government resolution said that both Hindi and English shall continue as official languages. Therefore, neither English nor Hindi was made the national language. India doesn't have a national language. India is a multilingual nation and that's the idea embedded in the Constitution. However, English and Hindi were given the status of official languages. The meaning of the term 'official language' is that, when one state converses with the other states, or when one state converses with the Centre, the state will have the freedom to choose either English or Hindi for that communication. That is the beginning and end of the meaning of the term 'official language'. The meaning does not extend beyond that interstate and federal communication for the purpose of governance. The term official language does not have any bearing or any rights on what language the citizens should use to speak or communicate in this country. The Constitution does not aim at regulating the languages that people use.

There is, however, an additional provision in our laws and as supported by the Constitution, in the rights, privileges and authorities given to the Governor. In order to protect a certain language, the Governor of a state can propose it to be added to the state's recognized languages. In India, there are thirty-six such languages recognized by different states. For instance, in Gujarat, in addition to Gujarati, the state recognizes Marathi as well as Urdu. In Maharashtra, the state recognizes in addition to Marathi, Sindhi, Urdu, Gujarati, and so on. Jharkhand state officially recognizes fourteen languages as official languages. The Centre's recognition of a language as official language is not expected to conflict with the recognition of any other official language of a state. This is the beauty of the Indian Union. India is a federation and a Union of States. These states which are linguistic states, primarily through the historical course of their becoming states, have the authority granted by the Constitution to decide which language or languages they want to recognize as official languages. However, when one state deliberates with another, which would be the language they would use? The 1974 formulation says they can choose to deliberate in English or Hindi. The meaning of this formulation does not extend beyond that at all. There are various Supreme Court Judgments allowing citizens to decide which language is one's mother tongue, which language one will use, to which school and medium of instruction individuals would like to send their children, and so on.

Until the beginning of the nineteenth century, when the books for the use of English administrators were printed in the government press in Calcutta, even the name Hindi was not used for the language that we today call as 'Hindi'. It had very many names including Khariboli, Avadhi, etc. But Hindi could connect several states in Central and Northern India with greater ease and therefore Hindi was put in the list of scheduled languages. But, is it the oldest, richest and most beautiful of all? About two years ago, a very ugly discussion surfaced in which a pro-Hindi politician made a deeply hurtful comment about Kannada. All languages, anywhere in the world, irrespective of the vastness of their vocabulary or heritage, are equally beautiful. No particular language is more beautiful or less beautiful than any other.

In the 2011 census, Hindi was reported to be spoken by 52 crore people in India. But, out of those 52 crore, there were many who did not speak Hindi as their mother tongue but only as a second language. For instance, Bhojpuri speakers had numbered about 5.03 crore in the same census. But they were clubbed together with Hindi. Similarly, Rajasthan has nearly forty-odd languages—small and big. All of them were grouped under Hindi. The languages of Himachal Pradesh, Uttarakhand, Bihar, Chhattisgarh, and Jharkhand were clubbed together with Hindi to inflate the figure for Hindi. There is a language native to the Pawra Adivasis of the Dhulia region in Maharashtra. Their language and Hindi are not mutually intelligible. A Pawra does not easily understand Hindi and it is far more difficult for a Hindi-speaker to understand the language of the Pawras. Yet, even the Pawra language was grouped under Hindi.

If we were to remove those sixty-six other languages that are forced to sit uncomfortably with Hindi, the number of Hindi speakers in India, according to the 2011 census would be 38 crore, against the base of 121 crore. This means that, 32 per cent people speak Hindi as their mother tongue. If India has more than 70 per cent people who don't speak Hindi as the mother tongue, the question of Hindi becoming the only official language and worse still, the national language of India, just doesn't arise.

Language is an enormously sentimental and contentious issue. In the post-independence past, people in Punjab, Maharashtra and Telangana, had waged struggles to get their linguistic states. And, many of the Scheduled Languages are among the most-spoken languages of the world. Out of 7,000 existing languages in the world, the first thirty include Bengali, along with Hindi, as well as Urdu, Marathi, Kannada, Tamil, Telugu, Malayalam, and Gujarati. There is no way that Hindi can be imposed on them or the speakers of these languages can be made to accept such an imposition. Never in its long history did India have any single 'pan-Indian national language'. India has always been multilingual and it is in the multilingual character of India that 'Indian-ness' can be located. It is distinct from the German-ness of the Germans, or the Italian-ness of the Italians. As of now, India has 850 living languages and every language matters since each one provides a unique world-view and people will be ready to fight for the preservation and dignity of their mother tongues. It is not that the central government does not know this. But dividing people along religious and linguistic lines and getting political mileage out of that division has become a political compulsion for electoral gains. Left to themselves, the Hindi-speakers may not be in favour of imposing Hindi on other language areas, nor may the English speakers in India be in favour of imposing it on the Hindi speakers. We are a multilingual nation as defined by the Constitution. That is the spirit in which we must go ahead in resisting the imposition of any Indian languages on any other Indian-language communities.

BIOLOGICAL EVOLUTION AND LANGUAGE FATIGUE

If democracy does not care for diversity, then it ceases to be a democracy. The heart of democracy is not in agreement, but in having space for debate, in having different views and different ways of looking at the world. This is not a situation unique only to India; rather it is prevalent all over the world. Papua New Guinea had a larger number of languages than India has. In 1961, it had claimed 1,100 languages; today it is not able to speak more than a few hundred languages. The same situation exists in Indonesia and Nigeria; in fact, India, Indonesia, Papua New Guinea, and Nigeria put together have about half of the world's languages in existence. But in all these countries with the maximum number of languages in existence, there is a huge amount of language deaths being reported. And what are the processes and consequences of the death of a language? When the last speaker stops speaking or when a large number of speakers migrate out of one language to another one, that's what makes a language disappear. For example, when the last speaker of the Bo language of the Andaman Islands, the Boa Senior Lady, passed away, the language died with her; similarly, when the last Majhi speaker in Sikkim died, the language also ceased to exist. But with the sinking of those words, a tradition of knowledge which has been in existence for thousands of years has also gone down. For some languages, this tradition of knowledge had been 70,000 years old. Occasionally, people inquire about the reasons behind the death of a language. Is the government alone responsible, or the education policy, or is it the poor quality of census that's responsible? Can it be perceived as an assault of globalisation? Or is it because of colonialism and its after-effects that the languages are in decline? Or can we blame the print technology for that matter? Beyond all these factors, there is a far more substantial explanation to these questions.

Humans have been an evolving species. In the process of that evolution during the last 500,000 years, humans had used only gestures for communication for most part of that long period. Subsequently, they began using tones, textures, and music for communication. But now it appears that humans are moving out of language and towards communication through images. The Broca's lobe is now showing great fatigue; children no longer wish to either read or write. All over the world, I believe, voice-based language is giving way to an image-based manner or system of communication. We are at a turning point in our evolutionary history. When we arrived at this turning point, since language was the foundation of knowledge, most fields of knowledge also started shifting their epistemic base. In fact, for quite some time now, new disciplines have been emerging, because the nature of knowledge is going to be very different in the coming years. However, we may continue to speak a few words but the ability of the words to carry their respective meaning will be much lower than what it is now. When knowledge is rapidly passing through a major epistemic shift, the state has a major role to play in terms of language policy. It is not sufficient for the state to just declare some awards or set up a few language-research institutions; there are numerous additional considerations about language that the state must address. Humans have amassed knowledge in language for the last 70,000 years through an enormous amount of labour. Each one of us has contributed to its development.

Experience accumulates. Then it stabilizes in cognition through verbal forms or even a pre-verbal but conscious sensation. These verbal forms are exchanged and transacted among the members of a community. Such transactions make the community possible as well. The two are interdependent.

Over a period of time, people discover, borrow, and, in some rare instances, invent methods of recording the cognition, as well as systems of representation such as orthography. Orthography is an expensive affair; it has been so all along. It takes several years for a person to acquire command over the rules and the restlessness of systems of representation. Therefore, records of human cognition easily tend to become the monopoly of a certain class which has the ability to buy leisure for their young ones so that they can 'learn'. This is where human learning and the 'learning' in a classroom part ways. History shows that classroom learning generates its own rhetoric to justify the sanctity of its superior cognitive content, more systematic than vulgar sensory experience, which in fact is the basis of all human knowledge. Subsequently, this rhetoric acquires the status of the basic principles in knowledge-systems such as logic, rationality, veracity, and so on. Human history is, in a way, a story of conflict between learning and experience, between the rational and the imaginative, between the left and the right halves of the brain. Knowledge, therefore, is a way of repression. Conservation or preservation of languages needs to be seen as being significantly different from the preservation of monuments. Languages are, as every student of Linguistics knows, social systems. They get impacted by all other contextual social developments. Language as a social system has an objective existence, in the sense that dictionaries and grammars of languages can be prepared, and languages can be transcribed, orthographed, mimeographed, and recorded on a tape by way of documents and objects, but essentially language does not have an existence entirely free of the human consciousness. Therefore, a given language cannot be completely dissociated from the community that uses it. Quite logically, therefore, preservation of a language entails the preservation of the community that puts that language in circulation.

Between the collective consciousness of a given community, and the language it uses to articulate the consciousness, is situated what is described as the 'world-view' of that community. Preservation of a language involves, therefore, respecting the world-view of the given speech-community. Most of the Adivasi communities believe that human destiny is to belong to the earth and not to offend it by claiming that it belongs to humans. Languages of the communities which have such a world-view do not have much of a chance of survival if they are forced to internalize a political imagination which considers vandalizing the earth's resources as a development norm and a prerogative of man. In such a situation, the community will have only two options: it can either reject the utopia that asserts the human right to exploit the natural resources and turn them into exclusively commercial commodities, or it can reject its own world-view and step out of the language system that binds it with the world-view.

The situation of the languages in the world, more particularly the languages of indigenous peoples, marginalized and minority communities, and of the cultures that have experienced or continue to experience alien cultural domination has become precarious. The alarm to be raised would not be even a day too early. Yet, it would be ambitious to hope that this task can be achieved even in a small degree by merely placing the onus and the responsibility on the state parties. The mission will have to be carried out through the agency of the nation-states and independent of it, through a large number of civil society actors—universities, literary and linguistic academies, good-will societies and associations, non-governmental organizations, individual scholars, researchers, and activists. Creation of texts, dictionaries, glossaries, and grammars in the declining languages will be of use; documentation, museumization and archiving too will be of some use, but if the languages are expected to survive, the speech communities need to be given the dignity and respect that they deserve, not as anthropological 'others', not as the last and under-developed traces of the self, but in their own right as deserving of respect because of what they are. It takes centuries for a community to create a language. All languages created by human communities are our collective cultural heritage.

3

MEMORY AND ORAL TRADITIONS

MEMORY AND ORAL TRADITIONS
Throughout human history, man has attempted to develop methods of representation of the natural phenomena by using various ingenious ways of encrypting the formal features of the phenomena. These attempts, from the ancient Egyptian hieroglyphs to the Greek trigonometry and the medieval European magical-code languages, had essentially aimed at storing human experiences in ways that would make them 'portable', giving them life beyond their natural life. The desire to represent, store, transact and to pass on to the succeeding generations what humans 'know' culminated in the seventeenth century French thinker Leibniz's conceptualization of a 'pure language', a language of signs that do not have any meaning at all by themselves but have the ability to represent constant and entirely non-subjective meanings (as in mathematical symbols). This was his 'logical calculi' (Paulo Rossi, 2006, p. 185). His attempt was preceded by a number of similar attempts made towards exploring methods of representing ideas and arriving at abstractions. During the historical phase of the transition from the use of Latin to that of the modern European languages for intellectual

and imaginative expression, more particularly the sixteenth and the seventeenth centuries, the obsessive attraction for inventing a symbolic method for 'stating knowledge' made it possible for European scholars to arrive at sorting ideas in terms of what came to be accepted as 'universal science.' Thus, in 1582, Giordano Bruno came up with the idea, as summarized by his commentator Paulo Rossi, that combining 'associations of ideas' in manageable symbolic strings would help to hold a vast amount of knowledge in a relatively small band of human memory.

Through the artificial retention of the 'chains' (or relations between the 'shadows') in the mind, one can reconstruct, by means of a gradual process of purification, the connections which exist between the ideas themselves. The contemplation of the unity which is hidden in the confused plurality of appearances leads to a rational understanding of ideal relations (Rossi, 2006). In 1675, a century later, Leibniz proposed his celebrated aphorism *'existere nihil aliud esse quam harmonicum esse'*: 'to exist is nothing other than to be harmonious' (Rossi, 2006, p. 192). In that span of a century and a half, from Bruno to Leibniz, Europe had discovered the ability of the human mind to reduce diverse perception to a 'harmonized understanding' capable of being stated in abstract terms. This ability is what is described in philosophical terms as 'rationality.' If Rene Descartes (1595–1650) gave to Europe the philosophical basis for its rationality, often highlighted through his claim *'je pense, donc je suis'* (I am, because I think), Bruno, Leibniz and their contemporaries gave Europe the method of stabilizing knowledge on the bedrock of rationality. These historical factors would not be of any direct relevance to an analysis of the trajectory of knowledge in India, or any other civilization, had it not been for the fact that they clearly point to the use of memory for encrypting and classifying knowledge. The history of 'sorting out and storing ideas' in Europe is also of interest to us, as in the process, memory gets completely transmuted from being just a commonly shared heritage of human societies to a higher order platform for commanding and canonizing the cerebral acts of humans. This results in the idea of a universal knowledge, or the real business of universities.

In Indian traditions of learning, memory had been a central interest from the earliest times. In fact, what was worth learning was described by the term *smriti* ('remembering' as well as 'the remembered'). The Bhagavad Gita contains a rather categorical pronouncement that the weakening of *smriti* leads to destruction of the intellect, *smriti-branshat buddhi-nash*. In ancient Indian literature and theoretical compositions, special care was taken to aid and facilitate easy remembering of the text by introducing various accessible mnemonic tools, quite akin to the Ciceronian use of memory. The larger part of the ancient Indian literature, of diverse philosophical schools, was preserved through memorization with a very high standard of accuracy. There is no other civilization in the world that insisted on developing memory as the most central tool of learning with such obsessive interest as was done in India for millennia. Probably, the difference between the turn that the seventeenth-century use of memory took in Europe and the use of memory in the history of ideas in India was that the idea of a 'science of knowledge, or a universal knowledge' did not find favour with those who held knowledge.

The idea of knowledge as 'knowing', bringing intellect closer to intuition, together with the sophisticated use of memory for a flawless reproduction of the texts from the past, had resulted in 'apprenticeship' becoming, as stated earlier, the most favoured mode of receiving and giving education in India. It was favoured not only for those disciplines such as medicine, chemistry, sculpture, architecture, metallurgy, dance, music and crafts, in which skills constitute the major part of understanding, but also for the disciplines which had the ability for abstraction and raising new questions from their core, such as philosophy, poetry, mathematics and astronomy. In combination with the social segregation that was entrenched in the Indian society more than two thousand years ago, the internship mode of cultivating knowledge became a formidable hindrance in producing any genuine 'universal science'. While a high-accuracy memorization continued to be the tool for storing developments in ideas, the access to such memorization was restricted by the social status of a person. The result was that in the pre-colonial times two broad streams of memory-based knowledge spectrums continued to coexist without much of a possibility for mutual exchange and cross-fertilisation: one, the spectrum of the memory traditions of those who had access to abstract symbols, including writing, and two, the spectrum of the memory traditions of those who were prevented from attempting symbolic abstractions.

In India's literary past, most of the linguistic creativity has been in the oral tradition. Though people knew how to write, writing was not used as a means of educating the next generation in remembering these compositions. This is not to deny that we had something written even in Harappan times, and also a tremendous era of literary productivity in ancient Tamil and post-Vedic Sanskrit, but by and large, knowledge, literature, and memory were handed down not through writing but through speech and oral media. What developed in India as oral tradition was not just 'writing' on walls, textile surfaces, and in figurative ritual designs, but also compositions of texts, document or what one describes as 'manuscripts'. They follow the logic of speech and the logic of orthography. The aim here is not in any way to establish writing as redundant but only to indicate that considering what is non-written as non-manuscript would be inadequate in accounting for India's 'knowledge' traditions.

Towards the beginning of the nineteenth century, when printing technology started giving new life to Indian languages, the status of knowledge in the non-printed and non-written languages diminished altogether. As a result, the split between the social sections who had easy access to letters and those who were denied that ease of access was aggravated at that precious moment of India's transition from medieval times to modernity. This is not to say that all the oral traditions of memory and knowledge in the non-printed languages ceased to exist at once. But, while they continued to exist within their limited confines, the possibility of India devising a grand scheme for classifying all that was known in Indian traditions with the help of a single and unified symbolic grid tied firmly to 'all memory'—as it had happened a couple of centuries ago in Europe—was no longer a viable possibility.

Under the impact of the colonial understanding of 'knowledge', Indians started looking at literature in terms of a binary division of 'literature' (which is available in written form) and 'folk-literature' (which is deprived of the opportunity of being written). While Indians had been building houses all along, architecture was divided in terms of 'vernacular' and 'architecture'. Languages, spoken as 'languages', came to be listed separately as 'languages' and 'dialect'. It is with the wound of a deeply divided 'memory field' that India has been trying to internalize the idea of a 'universal knowledge' over the last two centuries. The modernizing India of the nineteenth century had to launch the project of creating a society operating within a shared band of abstract signs welded to memory before it would start thinking of generating new fields of knowledge that qualified to be 'universal' science or discipline.

The historical juncture at which India started internalizing a pervasive cultural amnesia was also the moment in European history of ideas when memory started being seen as secondary or inferior to imagination. First Immanuel Kant in Germany and then Samuel Taylor Coleridge in England postulated memory as the 'agency which plays with mere tokens of fancy' while imagination, in this view, was the 'regenerative' power of the mind (Coleridge, 1817). In the words of an able commentator on this Romantic epistemology, M. H. Abrams, memory performed the function of 'a mirror', imagination that of 'a lamp'. Prior to this, the seventeenth-century philosopher Hobbes had spoken of imagination as a demonic force, born of melancholia, inducing in the mind 'fancy' of 'ghosts, goblins, witches, where they exist none'. (Hobbes, 1651). He had, in turn, derived the idea of imagination as a dangerous mental process from the ancient Greeks, particularly Plato. But the German and British Romantic poets of the nineteenth century started questioning the idea, using Plato again, and Plotinus. In sharp contrast to the disapproval of imagination that their predecessors had expressed, they proposed not imagination but memory as the spiritual-inferior, a game of empty tokens. They proposed imagination as an order of reality higher than the mundane and, therefore, with a superior truth value. William Blake stated unequivocally that 'whatever the imagination seizes as Truth exists, whether it existed before or not' (Blake, 1808).

Nearly half-a-century later, memory returned very powerfully as the centre-piece in the Freudian narrative of the human mind, the psyche. It was so central to Sigmund Freud's analysis of mental illnesses that had memory not been available to him, the entire edifice on which his psychoanalysis is based would have simply been impossible to construct. History of ideas often witnesses emergence of two completely antagonistic and competing thoughts or impulses, both of which keep evolving simultaneously. However, this need not be seen as an instance of Hegelian dialectics. During the nineteenth century, Hegel's theory of history, Marx's theory of material dialectics, and Freud's psychoanalysis made memory, in the structured and narrated form of history, their main ploy. This was too close in history to the rise of the camera technology, leading half-a-century later to the rise of cinema as the twentieth century's most powerful collective of image, fantasy, and dream. By the end of the century, the image-making devices and image-processing technology have brought to the world an alternative that appears to have started transforming human existence most fundamentally. The British Romantic poet William Wordsworth had made the quest for the lost 'spots of time' his poetic mission. In his view the 'spot' could unite time and space in a pure form. The recent discovery of 'digit' as the vehicle of knowledge is, in an ironic way, the technological culmination of that quest. The digit is now being conveyed over unimaginably long distances through electro-magnetic waves. The electronic digit has started impacting the world as nothing else in the human past ever has. In a relatively short span of time, the world as humans have known for the last half-a-million human years, and what Immanuel Kant described as the 'phenomenal world', is close to an irrevocable convergence with the digital world. The earliest symptom of the new convergence between the physical and the digital is the near-complete alienation of memory.

At present, most members of the human species have started depending on external memory-chips for performing the memory functions, which they had been performing by themselves during all the preceding generations. During the earliest phases of the long process of evolution of the human species, memory had been purely the individual's prerogative. Later, the collective memory, placed in the social space, assumed the form of schools. Paolo Rossi's fascinating classic, *Logic and the Art of Memory* (2006), on this theme, presents a complete account of the evolution of memory. During the European Enlightenment, a new order of memory in this collective space appeared as university, museum, and library, in turn, offering an 'objective' basis for disciplines of the 'universal knowledge'. In the present time, with the near-complete alienation of memory from humans, that basis of 'objective knowledge' is rapidly eroding. In its place, image is acquiring a greater power as the maker of knowledge. I shall use the term 'post-memory knowledge' for describing this new field that the human mind is engrossed in shaping. The post-memory knowledge is being 'written' through digital signs that can take meaning beyond the grammatical structures constrained by tenses (as the memory-based knowledge was).

Given that the human brain is constantly evolving and, in the process, has been acquiring untold powers to comprehend very complex realities, it is but to be expected that it forces the human language/s and thought to go beyond the established logic of tense and distance, beyond memory and imagination, beyond time and space, so that a far more complex multi-frame reality can be comprehended and expressed by humans through whatever means they will in future. Michael C. Corballis, in a fascinating study of the recursive brain of humans, offers an unsettling argument—that while the functions and the structure of the human brain are recursive, the structure of language is not so:

> The unique properties of grammar may have originated in the uniqueness of human mental travel... But the structure of language itself is not a matter of mental travel... Thus although language may have evolved, initially at least, for the communication of episodic information, it is itself a robust system embedded in the more secure vaults of semantic and implicit memory. It has taken over large areas of our memory systems, and indeed our brain (Corballis, 2011).

It is not unlikely then that when the pact between memory and the brain, or the one between language and the brain, is snapped, the brain shall figure out newer ways of 'thinking'. Perhaps, the imagination may occupy the areas of the brain functions that memory has occupied through a larger part of the human evolution.

NON-LEXICAL/ ORAL LANGUAGES

The use of oral practices in India just cannot be reduced to a question of pedagogy alone. The social and cultural context of oral expression is deeply rooted in the long history of over two thousand years of social exclusion of a large part of the society from knowledge transactions on the basis of sanction to write, granted to only a small section of society. My attempt here is to present at least synoptically the history of how the oral was reduced to 'non-knowledge', and how and why the current educational practice is heavily biased against oral practices. Therefore, it offers description of the language profusion and the complexity of interrelations between languages seen as 'superior' and 'inferior'.

History of oral practices in every civilization is directly impacted by the evolution of scripts and their use in knowledge transactions. Use of script goes back in Indian history to the third millennium BCE. The Indus civilization had what is believed to be a script. Archaeologists have made numerous attempts to decipher it. However, there is no conclusive reconstruction of the Indus script. Therefore, it has not become possible to decipher the texts on tablets and earthenware found during excavation. There is a conspicuous lack of scientific evidence about the period between the end of the Indus civilization and the emergence of the known ancient history of India. For nearly twelve centuries, after the Indo-Aryan language became the primary language of literary compositions, there is practically no evidence of the use of script or writing in India's history. It would therefore be appropriate to maintain that the known traditions of languages extend back to the second millennium BCE. The earliest literary compositions date back to some 3,500 years before our time. The method used for carrying them forward from generation to generation was a fully defined oral rendition. Education, if it is understood as inter-generational knowledge transaction, was entirely in oral forms.

Some two millennia before our time, philosophical and poetic texts were composed and taught in India in Sanskrit and Tamil using oral methods. The period of a pupil's internship with the teacher varied from case to case, but it is certain that oral instruction by the teacher and memorization of massive chunks of literature was the only available method of education at that time. Skills related to pottery, textile-making, agriculture, medicine, metallurgy, navigation, and animal breeding were passed down through hands-on learning and apprenticeship. Use of scripts and writing available oral compositions picked up during the fourth century BC, leading to periodic re-writing of those manuscripts in order to keep them alive. That practice continued unbroken till the thirteenth century. However, while writing became a part of school education, rewriting of manuscripts or writing one's own composition was not for everyone. Only the most skilled did so, others carrying on all knowledge transaction through oral means alone.

The use of paper as a material for writing emerged during the thirteenth century and that practice continued till the beginning of the nineteenth century. It continued, though changed radically, after printing technology arrived in India towards the end of the eighteenth century. At the time, despite the profusion of oral compositions and oral traditions which existed in numerous languages with a long lineage, printing became available only in a very few languages such as Bangla, Marathi, Kannada, Malayalam, Telugu, Hindi, and Gujarati. By the end of the nineteenth century, the colonial British government had established an educational system which had the written text at its centre and which linked writing skills with well-paid occupations such as law, medicine, and government positions. The result was that the languages with oral traditions came to be seen as inferior languages, not fit for knowledge transactions, and therefore not of use in schooling. The languages that had printed texts in them acquired a high social status and education in them acquired value. This turn of things also meant that the conceptual framework of knowledge would shift accordingly. A major historical landmark indicating the shift was the establishment of the Asiatic Society by the late eighteenth century British administrator-scholar Sir William Jones.

Since the times of Jones, major attempts have been made to propose and formulate conceptual categories for describing the biocultural diversity and knowledge traditions in India (Devy, 2017). The corresponding process of de-colonization, too, has produced attempts at synchronization of traditional knowledge with the colonial production of knowledge within the context of Western modernity. While the clash as well as collaboration between what is seen as knowledge compatible with the Western cognitive categories and knowledge traditions rooted in the lives of predominantly oral communities continue to occupy the imaginative transactions in India. The mainstream institutions of knowledge—such as schools, universities, hospitals, courts, etc.—have acquired forms that often leave out the complexities involved in the 'great transition of civilization in the Indian sub-continent'. Probably, the most important among the cognitive categories that continue to carry the stress of this 'transition in civilization' belong to the field of creative expression in language and language description. Decolonization of Indian aesthetics and Indian linguistics, without an obscurantist turning back entirely to the past, is the larger task at hand for the contemporary Indian intellectual, attempted several times over but not yet accomplished.

THE ORAL IN LITERARY HISTORY
The multiplicity of languages and a long literary past of three millennia make literary historiography in India a daunting task. The span of literary past of varied length for different languages poses yet another difficulty. The Eighth Schedule of the constitution lists only twenty-two languages at present. But I am thinking of all the languages in India, including those which became extinct and have or had literature produced in one form or the other. How does one approach in this regard the question of constructing a truthful, authentic, viable, pragmatic, functional, proper, and a descriptive history or a focused history? How does one construct any type of history or histories at all? Writing the history of English literature in England is like maintaining a garden where you know the names of all the species, the age of plants, blossoming seasons and the fruits to be expected. This is not to say that England's literary historiography has no challenges, yet attempting to do so is humanly possible. But Indian historiography is like entering the mythical 'Naimisaranya', where there is no beginning or end in sight. No single description will be entirely 'reasonable' in Indian literary historiography.

When analysing literary history one can find a terrible mix-up between the oral and the written. Further, that mix-up is guided, conditioned, or distorted by what I have called 'amnesia'. All our important literature in the past was produced, received, circulated, and remembered orally.

Writing became an established practice after the arrival of printing technology during the colonial period. I am not talking about Vedic literature, liturgical literature or texts as such. Imagine the fourth- and fifth-century plays which were produced orally. These plays were never read by people as there was no paper available. Texts were circulated through oral means. This was also helpful for the perpetuation of *sangeet* (music) tradition.

Mahabharata is a good example of a typical linguistic composition of traditional Indian literary texts. It is one great epic, like that of Homer, as it also passed from one generation to another in the oral tradition, but the Indian epic is accommodative of many languages. A single text in many languages was popular then, very much part of tradition. Think of playwrights—Shudraka, Kalidasa, or even those later-day and more 'sophisticated' playwrights—who invariably knew several languages. One of the theoreticians (in Sanskrit poetics) while looking at various literatures said that there are so many *Ritis* and proposed the *Riti Sidhanta*. Thus literature could be composed at once in any number of ways in any number of languages.

There is a little story about the mother of all stories in this country—*Kathasaritsagara* (Brihat Katha). Siva and Parvati often indulge in the business of storytelling. Parvati always likes new stories to be created for her. She therefore complains to her divine consort busy in responding to his devotees at the cost of neglecting her. Siva takes up the challenge of creating a new story exclusively for her. Parvati insists that the story should be only for her and nobody else and demands an exclusive story-telling session. So they create a special bower for her to listen to the story in isolation. But two of the Ganas attempt eavesdropping, curious to know what Siva was telling Parvati. She notices the two intruders and curses them with complete amnesia: 'You'll be born in another form and you will forget all these wonderful stories'. They appeal to Siva and out of his generosity, he softens the curse for them. There will be a possibility of recollection of what they forget, however, that will be a sad thing in their lives. These two are born as human beings: Vararuchi and Gunadhya. Vararuchi starts remembering these stories as Siva said, but in a Paisachik language and not in Sanskrit. The moment he remembers he wants to write down the stories. He catches hold of an animal, and since he has no ink and pen, he cuts the animal and with a sharp instrument dipped in the blood of the animal, he starts writing on the skin of the animal. Gunadhya, his companion, recites the stories. One is formulated in the written tradition and the other in the oral tradition. They take the stories to the King asking him for patronage. The King sends them back because the stories they have brought are in the Paisachik language and not in Sanskrit. Heartbroken, they return to the forest and start burning the stories one after the other. But Gunadhya wants to read them out before they are destroyed, and is heard by all the animals and birds. They come and eagerly listen to his charming stories. The animals and birds forget to drink and eat. They become thin and one such lean bird was served for lunch at the King's court. The King became angry and asked, 'How come there is no food in my kingdom?'

Somebody tells him about the recital of the stories in the forest and that all the animals and birds had forgotten to eat. The King rushes to the forest and saves the remaining part of the manuscript from the fire. The story in the Paisachik language also becomes a great story in the Sanskrit language. Several texts come together in it. The oral and the written stay together in our tradition. This happened everywhere in India—equally so in Kerala, in Assam, and elsewhere.

Because we had our own ways of remembering the past, our own styles of historiography, we decided that certain texts could be reinterpreted, rendered differently from time to time. An original text could be brought back to life in the form of translation. So translation was never looked down upon when compared with the original. The translation and the original were accorded the same importance. The translation was not treated as though it fell from paradise into the inferno. Dnyaneshwar (1275–1296) translated the Gita from Sanskrit to Marathi. *Dnyaneshwari* (Dnyaneshwar's commentary on the Gita) was also worshipped by people. Prakrit was not seen as secondary to Sanskrit. The oral was not treated as secondary to the written. Writing was not treated as sacred, but the oral was. *Vacha*/speech was some kind of a goddess. Even Sanskrit was written, in various times, in three different scripts. So a particular form of writing was not so important. If we look at the issue of writing from a sociological point of view (the history of the origin of societies) we find that writing emerged when agrarian societies started moving towards an early capitalistic aspiration, when there was accumulation of surplus. Imagine yourself in the age of the pastorals slowly moving towards becoming an agrarian society, then to semi-industrial, industrial, capitalistic, and now to global capitalistic.

SPEECH AND SCRIPT
Scripts, though conventionally wedded to their respective languages, have no logical relation whatever with the languages they represent. A given language is never dependent for its growth or decline on the script in which it is written. Having a well-developed script does not ensure superiority of a given language over other languages. A language can never be considered lacking in valuable aspects if it has not developed a script for itself. For example, the English language does not have a script of its own till today. English uses the Roman script. Yet, it is a mighty language. We cannot dismiss it as a dialect of Latin.

No script is a perfect representation of vocal symbols, graphic symbols and orthographic symbols. That's why when you write in your own language or English there are so many sounds that are difficult to be represented and you make many compromises. Each written script establishes a convention. Suppose, when I say, 'Rama is the King of Travancore', the way I write the word Rama in the regional script establishes a convention. One learns to associate the sounds with the graphical symbols. They are not quantitatively equivalent to verbal signals. Hence any script can represent any language. Many languages have fared well without having scripts for themselves.

When the British arrived in this country, we decided that

the written is more important than the oral. India started using paper in the thirteenth century. The Turkish paper merchants in Delhi had become extremely prosperous. That was the time when the oral traditions started being committed to written forms. For instance, in the days of Tukaram, the Marathi poet, the practice was this: a poet would write something and the writing was copied in different versions as printing was not possible. In those days copies were pretty expensive. Writings on paper/manuscripts/copies, according to certain reports, were sold and purchased for thousands of rupees. That's the time when excellent orthography was cultivated. Good handwriting became a value in education, which has now disappeared with the introduction of computers. A poet would write as well as sing his poems. The dramatist wrote some of the play but the actual presentation would be quite different. People heard the poems in the oral form while the written forms were also available. It is said about Tukaram that his enemies found it difficult to tolerate his rising stature and popularity. They decided to collect all his works and immerse them in the river Indrayani. After some days those bundles of papers surfaced. But the fact of the matter is that while the poems were written down, they were also circulated orally, and that is how society came to remember Tukaram's poems. We have a lovely story about the much later-day poet Ghalib (1997-1869). Towards the last years of his life, he used to write verses, but could not keep track of where he placed them. Once, while walking along the Ganga, he heard a beggar singing one of his poems. Ghalib had tears in his eyes. Deeply moved, he asked, 'Where did you find this?' The beggar held up a paper and replied, 'I've got this.' Ghalib did not have a record of the song himself. So the oral and the written existed together. When the British arrived in this country, the written became sacred.

The sacredness of the written originates not in the attitude of the British to writing or the oral. It originates in the British system of land records. Land ownership had to be written and all those series of land laws from 1763 onwards strengthened the idea that in order to establish one's identity and legal existence, one had to have something in writing as a testimony. At the end of the eighteenth century, we accepted the new colonial legal system. So many Indian languages were put to script (print media) then. The colonial government appointed one Lalluji Lal (1763–1835) at St. Fort Williams in Calcutta to create scripts for Indian languages or use available scripts. Most Indian scripts were based on Brahmi. Lalluji Lal put only some languages to print. He did not go round the country to find out which language was spoken by more people, which language has a better future, which one was old, which was eminent and so on. It was not a rational study; he decided entirely subjectively and put some of the Indian languages to print. Literature started being printed in those languages alone.

When we became independent, the Government of India prepared a schedule of languages, the Eighth Schedule of the Constitution, in which only those languages put to script by the British were listed. States were given to only those languages which had come in print. As a result of that we have linguistic states in the country. But there are language groups distributed on the borders of the states—people of different languages scattered on both sides. Look at the Adivasis—the Bhils, Gonds, Santhals, Mundas—distributed in four states. The Bhils are scattered in Maharashtra, Madhya Pradesh, Rajasthan, and Gujarat; Gonds in Maharashtra, Madhya Pradesh, and Chhattisgarh; Santals in Bengal, Jharkhand, Bihar, and Odisha. Because their languages were not in print, these people got scattered in different states of the country. It was not their fault, and not because they did not have a literary past. It happened because of colonial intervention.

In the Parliament of India only 4 per cent of Indian languages are heard and the remaining 96 per cent are not. Each language presents a world-view. It combines a community's imagination as well as memory. Each language is a unique world. Let me describe how imagination and memory combine in a language. The consciousness—supported by the sensory capabilities of the human body in time and space—makes sense of the world only through constant encounter with time and space. It is imagination which helps us through a series of images to organize space. Images of external objects keep bombarding our mind through the eye and the mind, and organize them as a created replica of the space. That's why imagination is important. About memory: humans have conceptualized time unlike other animals. Only the human animal speaks in a complex language. Other animals can refer only to the present—a dog or a dolphin may have limited memory. Humans, on the other hand, have conceptualized time, and complex time at that. Some Indian languages have six varieties of the past tense, some have four. If a language has six forms of the past tense, there can be at least six different approaches of looking at the past, six measurements of the time past. It has taken a very long time for human beings to arrive at the formulation of the past tense. The present tense was easy. The present tense refers to 'fact or truth', and the past tense tells 'a memory impression or fiction'. Telling 'an imagined memory' demands a much more complicated working of the brain. In the evolutionary history of language it has taken nearly 200,000 years or so for the humans to formulate something in the past tense.

When we first conceptualized time, in order to come to terms with it, we devised the past tense in language. If we had no memory we would not have been able to manage the past. I remember today that I am the same person as I was yesterday. It is through memory that I am able to put together the past and the present, and to create a sense of continuity in existence. Language functions with the help of imagination and memory. Every language organizes the world in its own terms, in terms of its own unique interpretation of space and time. In this, country when we lose about 96 per cent of our languages, we lose so much of our stock of world-views. In other words, we lose almost our entire intellectual capital on which a historiography of India can be created. It is time for us to look at these issues once again with alertness, by rearranging the conceptual categories which are given to us, and which we seem to have accepted unquestioningly.

We were told some two hundred years ago, that Indians had no sense of history, that India had only a cyclical sense of history, and that Indian time ran in cycles. None of that is true. Think of Bhartrihari, the fourth-century grammarian who wrote a second book in order to help the readers of his grammar text *Vakyapadiya*. That book is known as *Kaalasamuddesh*—a comprehensive view on tenses or time. In *Kaalasamuddesh*, Bhartrihari maintains that time has various possibilities. One kind of time is like a fixed road. Time does not move, we are wayfarers who walk through it. The second description is that time is like a well from which we keep drawing out its own source, trying to phase it out, but time returns to the source. For the third description, he gives the example of a person who trains birds. The trainer ties very thin, invisible strings to the claws of a pigeon and pulls them, in order to train and control it. Bhartrihari maintains that time is like the trainer, and all of us birds. Time controls us, tells us how much we will fly. This is not a cyclical sense of time. Clearly, then, we have a linear sense of time—multiple time and dynamic time. This is only one example. In Chinese philosophy, Arabic sources, and Russian sources which produced histories and historiographies in print, we had a sense of different varieties of time.

Two hundred years ago, during the colonial period, Indians were often told by the English that we were more akin to animals that are devoid of historical consciousness rather than to an 'advanced' race like the British. We somehow accepted that version. Till today, many of us believe that history has come to us only after Hegel in Germany or Hobbes and Locke in England. The time has come for us to look at the question of what literature is, what the oral and the written are, and what this amnesia that we have accepted entails. Worst of all is the fact that we are 'sentencing' (I use this word quite advisedly) so many languages in this country, silencing them and imposing certain debilitating conditions on them. The Greek language evolved the term aphasia—loss of speech which happens because the brain cannot communicate with the speech organs, or the speech organs themselves are deficient. But there is a different kind of 'aphasia' where, in a country like ours, speaking a language is treated as the surest kind of backwardness. Severe aphasia is being imposed on a large number of Indian languages instead of being proud of them. It is time to rethink. If we fail to reconsider the truths of our history and life, what consequences might we face? Allow me to illustrate the answer through a story.

This story was written by Mahasweta Devi (1926–2016). In the Amaravati district in Maharashtra, there is a tribe called the Korkus. In the early 1990s, the Korkus started dying in large numbers due to sickle cell disease a genetic disorder, prevalent in the tribal communities in the country. The government of Maharashtra appointed a committee. The doctors went there and returned with the opinion that nothing could be done. I became aware of the ongoings. During the 1990s, I had started working with Mahasweta Devi on nomadic communities. I invited her to visit the Korku community in Amaravati. We went together and saw a devastated landscape. She came back and wrote the following story.

> When the Korkus realize that they will all die, they decide to die in a dignified fashion rather than mourn over their

predicament. They build a cottage and wait there to die when one's time comes. The last of the Korkus, Mahadu (Mahadev), a young boy, waits in the cottage to die. A doctor who has done extensive research on the effects of malnutrition visits Mahadu and administers a fluid known for its efficacy in ameliorating the symptoms of sickle cell disease. Observing Mahadu's improved health condition following the injection, the doctor acknowledges the positive impact of the treatment. The doctor immediately leaves for Geneva to present a paper, in a science conference, on the success of his invention. But Mahadu is waiting in the cottage, hungry and alone. The Korku forest was given away to the British for constructing the wooden sleepers—logs put under the railway tracks. The railway line from Howrah to Surat is made of the Korku trees. Mahadu, while waiting in the cottage, hears the whistle of a train and suddenly senses the fragrance from the past that pervades one's senses; it comes from the timber snatched away from his ancestors. He rushes to the train and jumps into it. The train takes him to Bombay and there, lo and behold! He sees a strange thing: he sees food for the first time in his life. He feels hungry: he feels the hunger of generations. He starts eating and eats everything. Because there is not enough food for him in Bombay he starts eating the Victoria Terminal building, the Bombay University and many such tall structures of the city. His stature grows tall and his head touches the sky. Then he bends and drinks the

Arabian Sea, rises again, raises his hands and plucks the stars from the sky, and starts rewriting the history of the Korkus, a new history, new literature.

LANGUAGE ACTIVISM OF ADIVASIS

The 2011 census report indicated that the Bhili language group recorded an 85 per cent increase among the speakers, whereas the population increase in the corresponding geographical area was just about 15 per cent. Therefore, the figures for the speakers of Bhili need to be read together with the figures of the neighbouring main languages. When that is done, it becomes clear that nearly four million persons who had previously claimed either Gujarati or Marathi as their mother tongues—the languages of the states where they live—now claim one of the varieties of Bhili as their mother tongue. For a tribal/indigenous language, this increase is remarkable. It will be necessary to take into account the role played by a language-based development movement initiated by the Bhasha Research Centre's Adivasi Academy in that area over the last two decades. The movement placed the linguistic self-consciousness at the heart of the development programme initiated among the Adivasi communities. Nearly three hundred community workers were trained using the local language and the local idiom of development for intervening in over a thousand villages. Organic agriculture, traditional medicine and healthcare practices, folk-songs and oral narratives, local pedagogic conventions, Adivasi arts, and craft were brought to bear upon the developmental discourse in the area. At the Adivasi

Academy, higher educational courses were introduced for promoting alternate/green development. All these measures triggered a will to survive and a linguistic energy unmatched among other Adivasis in the country. There is now a greater understanding among tribal activists all over the country that tribal identity and culture cannot be preserved unless their languages and literature are foregrounded. Every continent has its own stories of the colonial experience, the marginalization of the indigenous, their struggles, and the emergence of their voice in the respective national literature. The first decade of the present century was marked in India by the emergence of the expression of the voice of the indigenous communities. Throughout the first decade there was a remarkable manifestation of this voice through little magazines in various languages. Previously, the literary creativity of the indigenous communities came to us solely through the recordings made by anthropologists, linguists and folklorists. Besides, the translations through which the folklore was rendered were largely unreadable. Perhaps, the only exception was of the works by Verrier Elwin. In a way, the imaginative life of the 'Janajatis'—as the official term likes to describe the indigenous people—or the Adivasis of India, has remained inaccessible to the rest of the country.

During the early part of the twentieth century when the Dalits started registering their voice in Indian literature, the Adivasis kept themselves entirely within the confines of their oral tradition of epics, stories, and songs. In fact, it took a sympathetic observer like Verrier Elwin to articulate on behalf of the Adivasis, for they remained quiet. Even after Independence, the fiction of the Adivasis had to find expression through the writings of Gopinath Mohanty and Mahasweta Devi, who were tremendously sympathetic to the plight of the Adivasis but were not Adivasis themselves. It is in this context that the Malayalam author Narayan's (1940–2022) *Kocharethi* acquires a tremendous historical significance. *Kocharethi,* written in 1988 and published in 1998 in Malayalam, is decidedly the first novel written by a person belonging to the tribal community in India. Indian literature has reason to celebrate the work not only as the first such novel but also as a remarkable literary achievement. It is important both as history and as literature. It is even more important to perceive it as paving the path for emerging voices of Adivasis all over the sub-continent. In our time, when the larger society is content in looking at the Adivasis as perennially marginalized, and when the state is in a way demonizing the discontent among the Adivasis, Narayan no doubt has accomplished the feat of building a crucial bridge.

In the stunningly rich tapestry of Indian literary creativity, an important strand has been the lyrical and dramatic traditions of Adivasi communities and the picaresque narratives constructed by the nomadic communities (Devy, 2003). In most cases, the literary works in the languages of India's Adivasi communities have been oral in nature. The number of languages in which Indian tribal communities have been expressing themselves is amazingly large. The reorganization of Indian states after Independence was along linguistic lines. The languages that had scripts came to be counted for. The ones that had not acquired scripts, and therefore need not have printed literature, did not get their own states. Schools and colleges were established only for the official languages. The ones without scripts, even if they had a stock of wisdom carried forward orally, were not fortunate enough to get dedicated educational institutions. It is in this context of gross neglect that one has to understand the creativity in the languages of India's Adivasi communities. Some four decades ago, when Dalit literature started drawing the nation's attention towards it, it was usual to include Adivasis and nomads among them as part of the Dalit movement. At that time, the Northeast was no more than a rumour for the rest of India. During the early 1990s, I decided to approach the languages such as Kunkna, Bhili, Gondi, Mizo, Garo, Santhali, Kinnauri, Garhwali, Dehwali, Warli, Pawri, and so on, expecting to find at the most a few hundred songs and stories in them. As a beginning of the work, my Adivasi colleagues and I launched a series of magazines in Adivasi languages. These languages included various subgroups of the Bhili family and a couple of languages of nomadic communities, such as Bhantu spoken by the Sansis and Gormati spoken by the Banjaras. I am now painfully aware of how little of the vast literary wealth my humble efforts have managed to tackle. If a systematic publication programme is created to document the oral tribal literature in India, several hundred titles containing the oral traditions could easily be launched.

Indian civilization is based on knowledge developed through oral traditions. However, during the course of history, the oral came to be perceived as inferior to the written word. Colonialism and the print technology have contributed further to this marginalization. As a result, the education system and knowledge transactions in India do not consider oral learning and oral reproduction of knowledge as viable modes of knowledge processing and knowledge production. The current state of the oral tradition is entirely bleak, though attempts are being made to restore to it the privilege that it deserves. This, however, is not the story of most of the indigenous languages in India. Nor is the situation very different in most of the Latin American, African, and Asian countries, where a few indigenous languages and cultures have been showing a great resilience, while others have been languishing in neglect and have lost the nerve and the desire to survive. Take, for instance, the case of the Nahuatl as reported by Gabriel Estrada:

> Nahuatl is an ancient indigenous language with Uto-Aztecan affiliations that now span from Central America to Canada. It has many dialects in Mexico, and is also linguistically related to the Pipil of El Salvador; the Wixarika, Cora, Yoeme, Coahuiltec, Raramuri, Opata, O'odham, and Tepehuan of Mexico; as well as the Hopi, Comanche, Coahuila, Paiute, Ute and Shoshone that stretch from Mexico north to Canada across the Western US. According to linguistic theory, these members may have shared a common past in the US Southwest before parting ways and evolving across North America....
>
> Nahuatl was a lingua-franca at the time of the Spanish Conquest in the sixteenth century and spoken

by tens of millions of indigenous peoples. According to the 1990 Mexican census 'speakers of all Nahuatl varieties' numbered 1,376,898 just ten years before the third millennium began (Gordon 2005). Today, Nahua communities struggle to maintain language in the face of urbanization, free-trade economies, and modern educational practices that continue to privilege popular culture and use of the Spanish language (Estrada, 2008).

As against the instance of Nahuatl is the case of the new life breathed among the Australian aborigines with the establishment of the 'Garma' as reported by Peter Phipps in 2009:

In 1999 Galarrwuy Yunupingu established the Garma Festival of Indigenous Culture with his equally famous brother Mandawuy, lead singer of the popular rock band Yothu Yindi. The Yunupingu brothers, both separately recognized as 'Australian of the Year', mobilized this unique cultural-political initiative under the organizational structure of the Yothu Yindi Foundation, supported by a shifting alliance of Yolngu clan groups, principally the Gumatj-Rirratjingu. These two brothers were perhaps uniquely well-qualified and resourced in Australia to breach the chasm of mainstream Australian ignorance of Indigenous realities and to make a cultural leap in the process of decolonization. Over the years Mandawuy Yunupingu's vibrant creativity and Galarrwuy's political momentum, both drawing on a very strong grounding in Yolngu cultural life and law (röm), had gathered together a well-connected network of talent and support from across Australia and a reservoir of goodwill particularly amongst educated urban 'southerners', as the population from the south-east of Australia is known 'up north'. Mandawuy had a university degree from 'down south', had been the first Indigenous school principal in Australia at the bilingual Yirrkala Community Education Centre, and his bi-cultural rock band had an international following which broke into the Australian mainstream with the overtly political hit-song Treaty in 1992 (Phipps, 2009).

LANGUAGE AND REALITY

The process of human evolution holds back many secrets from our understanding in such a manner that we may only build apparently scientific hypotheses about them: such hypotheses that even the exactly contrary positions may sound equally convincing. Language as a social institution, the nature of its exact origin, and the clear sequence in its formation, are some of the mysteries in the epic text of human evolution. Was there an attendant sound when the universe came into existence? Did sound exist at all prior to the development of the animal ability to perceive it? Do the 'eternal sound'—the *anahat dhvani*—and the sound produced by vocal chords belong to the same material type? Why did the human animal select regulation of breath by the vocal chords as the means for meaning transaction, when it could have possibly been equally effective with the human eye or through body movement (as honeybees do)? Why didn't the human animal cultivate those other means of expressions with an equal degree of obsession? All these questions can be answered at the theoretical level, but the answers do not cross the level of philosophical propositions that are neither true nor untrue, for they defy the test of veracity.

Once regulation of air by the vocal chords came to be the central mode of meaning transaction, and subsequently numerals and letters became the surrogates for sound, why was it that the script language did not entirely displace the sound language? While the theory of language acquisition inherent in the mind structure of an infant has been formulated, why has the theory of the natural ability to perceive the correspondence between those geometrical shapes called letters and the human sounds called syllables so far not been posited? 'Meaning' consists of the meaning expressed through gesticulations, sound regulation and script marks, as well as through silence and stillness beyond the pale of these three. What exactly constitutes meaning has not been conclusively determined. The theories of meaning have so far remained at the level of philosophical speculation. Besides, it has so far not been possible to state with any great precision as to whether meaning is language, or if meaning exists prior to language and is capable of transcending human language even when language is an experience within the range of perception of an individual. This has led us to conclude that language is a social institution. But is language 'meaning', is it some material, is it a transcendental energy or a purely social institution, or is it a mere biological function given to the human body in the process of evolution? Or is it all of these at once or in various aspects of the language phenomenon? All these questions need yet to be tackled fully, despite linguistics being one of the most developed of human sciences.

There is a well-established view that culture has no other expression but language, that the two are one and the same. It is maintained that cognition too would be impossible without language. A similar view on meaning too exists. In other words, for practically every transaction of the intellect, 'language' has been used as a synonym that determines the outer boundaries of each transaction of the intellect. Even when the structure of dreams is not based on language content, it is conceptualized as being the same as language structure. The origin of dreams is in the ability to remember, in memory. In other words, we are made to believe that memory cannot exist entirely in the absence of language. Similarly, we have come to believe that other psychic possibilities such as inspiration, imagination, and reason cannot exist in the absence of language. While these hypotheses seem unexceptionable, it is true that there are experiences that the human animal shares with other animals that show a marked absence of language based on sound regulation.

Vertigo, or the fear of falling, and love or sensuous attraction are the main instances of such experiences. Phenomenology, which is one of the sciences of human understanding, maintains that language develops in tune with the perpetually increasing scope of the phenomenon perceived by the human mind. As against this, it has been argued that the human grasp of the phenomenal reality increases in proportion to the ever-increasing ability of language to grasp complexities.

It is indeed difficult to establish if a domain of experience exists independently and outside the domain of language. At the same time, it is even more difficult to overrule the existence of such a domain of experience. Similarly complicated is the question of whether those semi-verbal or verbal substances that scripts, grammars, and cultures do not admit as language are language or not? At best they find a place in marginal categories such as dialects and regional varieties. In fact, in the vast spectrum of meaning beginning with the mysterious origin of sound, to its pervasive spread through human space and time, human languages may at best be seen as dialects of the uninterrupted *dhvani*. Similarly, in the total range of meaning capable of being conducted through material and symbolic means, the sound-symbol based language will have to be counted as a dialect of the total range of meaning. Moreover, the process of the perpetual increase in the human experience interlocked with language will have to be thought of as a dialect of the universe of experience. And the totality of the human languages stabilized through words and scripts will have to be seen as a dialect of totality of all experience, all meaning and all sound. Therefore, to be a dialect is not to be left behind, but to be the avant-garde, to be on the forefront. If we imagine a certain component of language (as a substance within the system that it is) whose destiny it is to be at the turbulent interface of the ever-expanding reality, and if we imagine that this component is required to persist in its work without losing its identity as language—be in currency at least with the value of the counterfeit—we will have adequately imagined a dialect. To use a metaphor, dialect is like the amorphous substance surrounding a newly born planet which is yet to find its ultimate rate of revolution. That planet environment of the language is defined by its dialects. It is through them that language keeps its ceaseless contact with the universe outside it, and therefore manages to belong to it.

4

DIGITAL FUTURE, TRANSLATION, AND KNOWLEDGE

TOWARDS A VIRTUAL WORLD

Humans all over the world tacitly are now willing to surrender human memory and replace it with the artificial memory chip. Humans are moving from that memory to this new memory system, and in the process trashing out, vandalizing, and giving up what has accumulated as memory. Think of it as a global phenomenon related to the process of evolution, where humans are capable of accommodating the virtual with the real. Though what has been imagined by humans to be 'real' is itself virtual as seen from a certain perspective of philosophy, there is another kind of virtual in relation to what we believe to be real; and we are trying to graft the two together. As we wish to sail effortlessly between the virtual and the real, in search of a new space, a new order of time, we are positive about the possibility and the outcome. In order to be humans, and not just machines, even in that virtual space and time (the conventional real and the new virtual clubbed together), if we wish to continue as humans and not robots, or cyberspace creatures, we will have to be extra sensitive towards the collective memory which our ancestors accumulated over the millennia. We have to be especially sensitive to the idea of diversity, which is at the heart of democracy. If humans merely become cyberspace creatures, or the masters of robots, and lose their diversity, dialogue and democracy, they will have rubbished the long process of their evolution and brought the species back to the status of being a mere animal—a machine animal. Languages and states are interlocked today in a fierce battle as the latter want to silence people through a pervasive surveillance—over speech and thoughts. The state is interested in introducing a kind of thought virus in the mind of citizens. Therefore, it is of utmost necessity to protect that space, of words, metaphors, euphoria, insanity, thought, and memory.

DECLINE OF INDIAN LANGUAGES

Despite the vast range of the existing linguistic diversity in India, and the official support that is being given to a relatively large number of languages, the language stock in the country has started showing signs of a rapid decline. Several historical factors appear to be responsible for the decline. The print technology impacted Indian languages profoundly during the nineteenth century. The languages that were printed acquired importance (Austen and McGill, 2011); the ones that remained untouched by it came to be seen more as dialects than as languages, though that was not the case in every instance. Subsequently, the process of state reorganization in the country invoked the principle that a language is a language only if it has printed literature in it. Obviously, the languages like Bhojpuri or Gondi, despite having large numbers of speakers were never considered for statehood and school education. The reorganization of Indian states mainly as linguistic states turned the already marginalized and 'non-printed' languages into 'minority' languages.

The death of a language is literally surrounded by silence. By its very nature, it cannot be visible, and so it fails to move anyone, except the very last speaker of that language nurturing an unrequited hope of response. When a language goes, it goes forever, taking with it knowledge gathered over centuries. Every instance of annihilation of natural creation does not require an all-sweeping tsunami to hit it. A bureaucrat's benign decision can as well cause it. Even a well-intentioned language census can do it. The existential pathos of the peoples whether identified from outside, or through self-identification as 'marginalized, minority, indigenous', has common features in all continents. The indigenous have been facing deprivation and dispossession of their natural resource base, denial of access to quality education, healthcare and other citizenship rights, and have come to be seen as 'a problem for the development project of modernity'. Going by any parameters of development, these communities always figure at the tail-end. The situation of the communities that have been pastoral or nomadic has been even worse.

Considering the immense odds against which these communities have had to survive, it is not short of a miracle that they have preserved their languages and continue to contribute to the astonishing linguistic diversity of the world. However, if the situation persists, the languages of the marginalized stand the risk of extinction. Aphasia seems to be their fate. It may not be inappropriate to assume that people all over the world are paying a heavy cost for a 'global' development in terms of their language heritage. This linguistic condition may be described as the condition of 'partial language acquisition' in which a fully literate person, with a relatively high degree of education, is able to read, write, and speak a language other than her/his mother tongue, but is able to only speak and not write the language she/he claims as the mother tongue.

SPEECH AND SCRIPT
Some years ago, I was working on a comprehensive survey of languages in India. The larger majority of the languages I was dealing with had been in oral traditions and without any writing conventions. It was surprising for me to find that several of those languages had folklore referring to the existence of writing in them. For instance, the language of the Rathwa community, an indigenous group in the western Indian state of Gujarat, has a well-developed style of painting. These paintings are done collectively over a period of three days as one of their propitiation rituals. The word for the master painter used in their language is 'lakhara', which literally means 'writer'. To my mind, conditioned to think of language manifestation as either 'speech' or 'writing', it seemed natural to infer that the paintings of the Rathwas were some kind of 'writing', and since these are paintings made on walls, literally as 'writing on the wall'.

In another instance, I came across a community called 'Gondhali' in western Maharashtra which had persons with an amazing skill to write in the air. This writing, given the ethereal nature of the medium, involved a simultaneous reading as well. The practice is as follows: one person (call him 'X') stands in open space at a given point. Imagine him to be the writer. Another matching person (call him 'Y') stands at a sufficiently long distance, say a hundred meters or so, so as not to be able to hear any normal utterance of the first person X. You are asked to whisper any sentence in any language into the ears of X. X then moves his arms, and Y utters the sentence you had given to X, exactly as you had said it. I checked very carefully to see if any distant-hearing electronic device was concealed anywhere close to X or hidden in his/her clothes. Having satisfied myself that there was no chance of trickery or deception, I asked them to repeat the performance, first using sentences in Marathi, then in Hindi and English. And finally, I asked some of my European visitors to try this out using their French and German languages. The results in all those trials were entirely satisfactory. This was amazing. The only conclusion I could draw was that the movements of hands that X did was a way of 'writing in the air' which Y could see and 'read'. The Gondhali community has followed this method of writing for several centuries and has ways of training the next generation in using this invisible 'script'. I have so far not done a video documentation of this script, as I am not sure if one can pry into what has been the intellectual property and an intangible heritage of a community.

In a third instance, I came across in the Northeastern state of Meghalaya a very widely shared belief that when humans were created, they were sent to dwell on the earth with letters as their clothes. On their way to the beautiful hills of Meghalaya, they had to cross a river. In order not to spoil the great gift given to them by the Maker, they took off the vestures and swam across, but the swirling rapids took away the clothes. So, they came out to the other side without their script. The allusion to writing, the varieties of imagining scripts and the script-fantasies are far too common among the speech communities, as yet far from developing their scripts, to be dismissed as an aberration arising out of a cultural hybrid. The most striking example, almost the prototype, of reference to writing embedded in oral traditions is found in the Mahabharata, the mother of all that is literature in India. It need not be stated here that the Mahabharata has been, in its 'textual tradition', an 'oral epic', something so beautifully captured by A. K. Ramanujan (1929–1993) when he stated that, 'Everybody in India knows the Mahabharata because nobody reads it.'

In the first 'Book' of the Mahabharata (the term understood by us literates as 'parva' also means unit of time or period), we are told that while the poet Vyasa, who recited the entire version for the first time, 'speaks out the verses' in a fit of poetic energy; Ganesh is asked to 'write down' the entire recitation as a faithful 'transcription'. At one point, when the stylus with which Ganesh is writing breaks, he just breaks one of his teeth (elephant tusks, really) and continues with his task. Within the Mahabharata lore, the broken tusk of Ganesh is the symbol of writing, trying to stay on par with the rapidity of the oral. However, any public recitation of the Mahabharata has to begin with a prayer to Ganesh, its 'scribe'. Many of the oral traditions in India thus recognize a pre-existent written, or simultaneity of the oral and the written, challenging the historiography of writing—that which is in letters, literature—as a temporal second to the oral. When this cultural habit, this negation of the gap between the preceding and the succeeding, is carried to the hermeneutics of translation, it opens up a question difficult to tackle.

THE NON-SEQUENTIAL 'IS-NESS' OF LANGUAGE

The question can be stated more clearly by referring to the theory of meaning in Indian tradition. One must add that there is not just one unified tradition of semantic philosophy in India. During its long history, several schools of Semantics emerged, held sway, became part of the popular thought and belief, and continued to survive in one or another form of thought. Though in most cases these were mutually complimentary, there were also the ones that conflicted in their orientations and competed with each other in claims to higher philosophical sophistication. Bhartrihari's *Vakyapadiya* composed in the fourth century CE and Anandavardhana's *Dhvanyaloka*, composed four centuries later, are generally held as being the most iconic and foundational texts in this area of inquiry. Bhartrihari conceptualized meaning in terms of *sphota* and Anadavardhana in terms of *dhvani*. Both use a multi-level description of word, a level that is seen and perceived, and another—one or more—level(s) perceived though not accessible to the immediate sensory experience. Both try to decide the question of the sequence of these levels in terms of the prior and subsequent or, if one were to use the Cartesian logic, the cause and the consequence.

Bhartrihari begins his analysis of the temporal spectrum of meaning by pointing out the limitations of the Grammarian school of philosophy—the *Vaiyakarans*:

> Grammarians consider that there are two 'word-entities' in functional words; one, i.e., the *sphota*, is the cause of the production of words and the other, the speech-sound, is used in connection with meanings. Some, among the teachers of old, considered that there was a difference in essence between these two. Others on the other hand speak of the same undivided entity being thought various, through a difference in conceiving it. Just as the light which is in the fire-stick acts as the cause for further lights, similarly the Word which is in the mind is the cause of speech-sounds. The Word is examined in the mind, is then fixed to a specific meaning and then through the instrumentality of the speech-sounds produced through their causes. The Word is neither a 'previous' nor 'a subsequent', because it is the speech sound which is produced in sequence (Devy, 2009).

The linguistic philosophers preceding Bhartrihari had conceptualized 'meaning', the preverbal stock of linguistic cognition, and meaning, the cognition resulting out of the perception of the verbal signs, as being of 'the same essence'. Bhartrihari challenged the idea by pointing out that rather than thinking of the two domains of meaning transactions as unified and one, it would be philosophically more appropriate to consider the two instances of their existence as belonging to a single temporal span. In other words, he proposed that the ideas of 'before' and 'after' do not apply to the process of meaning production as they apply to other material events. Instead, he proposed, it would be more useful to think of a different order of temporality in which there is neither a 'before' nor an 'after' but all is 'all time', forever and is just 'is'.

The non-sequential 'is-ness' of meaning in Bhartrihari's postulation pointed to the sanctity of the 'produced' meaning as against the 'given and a pre-existent pure and absolute'. Speech acts are neither less nor more than the semantic web from which they draw sustenance, though they may differ in their essential constitution. He uses a series of fascinating metaphors to draw home this point. For instance, he points out, the image of an object held over a stream is not the object, but the two coexist in the stream in an 'instance' without one being prior to the other. Causality in a given temporal framework would be of one kind, but would be more inconsequential if time were to be imagined differently. *Sphota* is in Bhartrihari's conception the listener's realization that the words one heard and understood and the meaning stock in one's mind that allows one to understand them thus, are capable of linking with each other on a different plane of time. One need not rush to add the epithet 'everlasting'. Bhartrihari was not discussing any 'everlasting time' as against 'ephemeral moments' in his *Vakyapadiya*. Rather, he was challenging the seemingly easy way of escape into metaphysics. He therefore brought to bear upon meaning the idea of a 'transfixed time', *sphota*, which helps the cognition to open into a different order of time and then to return from it to a normal temporality.

Bhartrihari's postulation is of importance to understanding translation not because of what he says about meaning but because of what he says about time. To return to my last sentence of the previous section, the 'difficult question' is not if the written is prior to, or subsequent or simultaneous with the oral, but if the written as well as the oral point to the need for imagining a different order of time. Before commenting any further on this, it would be useful for us to briefly allude to one of the earliest theoretical positions on translation in India that is to be found in the most widely mentioned, and the least studied doctrine, the *Natyashastra*. The term used by Bharatamuni—the author of the doctrine—is *anukarana*, which has been rendered into English as 'representation'. The translation of the term in English has the same kind of philosophical difficulties as the translation of Aristotle's *aporia*. However, without getting into any hair-splitting about the meaning—whether, in the specific context in which Bharata uses it, the term should mean 'interpretation', or 'representation', or 'losing oneself into the original'— let me move to the importance of Bharata's perspective for our purpose.

The primary aim of Bharata's treatise was to explain why and how we respond to theatre. In its opening sections, he claims, 'There is hardly any knowledge, any artist's craft, any lore, any fine art, any design, in which art, lore and emotions are interconnected, any activity, that will not be seen in *natya*' (Devy 2009). *Natya*, he goes on to claim is the 'nature and behaviour of the world'. The key term he uses in this postulation is *svabhava*, 'the very being' or 'nature without attributes'. A lot of what follows is an explanation of what makes *bhava*—representation of emotion into *svabhav*a—representation of the very nature of the world. In his elucidation of the process, he moves from the discussion of transient emotions—*vyabhichari* to permanent emotive states—*sthayi*; and concludes that the movement is a result of the viewer's ability to go beyond the self, to be a *sahrhidaya*.

Bharata's work draws its lasting quality not only from his ability to provide taxonomy of emotions. Many other lesser critics did this with a greater methodological rigour than him. It is also not based in his insights into the nature of human emotions. Rather, it lies in his ability to point to a process in human cognition that lifts the primary-level perception to an order of experience that transcends the framework set upon representation by the ordinary habits of mind. Seen from this perspective, it may not be inappropriate to suggest that the theory of representation by Bharata and the theory of meaning by Bhartrihari point to the need to look deeper into the process of how language is interpreted inside the human mind. They push us farther than what ordinary interpretative acts do towards looking at the recursive quality of the human brain. This is not to claim that they anticipate modern neurosciences. That would be too heavy a claim on too slender evidence. It is just that the ancient theories orient us to move ahead in that direction.

The recursive brain enables humans to produce speech and also to think about the speech produce, to retrieve meaning out of what is heard, and at the same time, to look at what is being heard as meaning. This peculiar ability of the human brain, as distinct from the brain structures of other living species, provides us with the mental mechanism to segregate language transactions into 'transactions as they happen' and 'transactions as one observes and analyses while they are happening'. Given the immense network of active neurons helping the language transactions within the human brain—some eighty-five billion of them—the 'thinking about thought' is an activity that takes place in the brain almost simultaneously with the activity of thinking. To use an everyday example, one knows what the other person is going to say even before the other person has uttered the full sentence. Similarly, one knows within one's mind the unstated parts of an utterance while the 'verbal formation of the statement' is still in process. In other words, the recursive brain simply makes mockery of our commonly shared ideas of the 'prior' and the 'subsequent'. To use Bhartrihari's insight for simplifying this concept for contemporary neuroscience, the language transaction within the human mind works in terms of *sphota*, with each individual word grasped as a symbolic token as well as those words collectively understood as a single spectrum of meaning, and not in terms of a lingering domino effect. To use this observation for translation, the original and the translated representation simply coexist in an order of time that is not the time perceived by us as historical time. Indeed, all of us are moving very rapidly to a phase of human expression in which the established notions of time will be entirely replaced by the flexible and simultaneous time(s). For the moment and since a term for it has not so far been coined, let me call this 'translation time'. Since it is a bit too early within our settled temporal framework to think of such a 'translation time', let me offer a somewhat elaborate overview of the process through which the human engagement with language has arrived at this juncture.

THE WHEEL AND THE SCALE
It has been a convention to depict on the cover page of the Bhagavad Gita the image of Arjuna on a chariot with Sri Krishna as the charioteer, one of his arms raised towards the skies, with one of his fingers supporting the *chakra*. The *chakra* is described in the ancient Indian mythology as Krishna's weapon, the ultimate weapon with an unmatched divine power and which has been gifted to Krishna alone. Though it is not quite clear if the Bhagavad Gita was a part of the Mahabharata from the earliest phase of the Mahabharata lore, when it was known as Jaya-Ithasa, or whether it was added to the ever-growing epic at some later period. What is clear though, is that the *chakra*—the wheel—has been at the heart of the Mahabharata story. This one is termed as the *kala-chakra*, indicating the inexorable flow of events in human time, the *kala*. There is no doubt that in its earliest form and in numerous regional versions in which the Mahabharata emerged and continued to exist throughout the

history, the plot of the epic is centred round an epoch-making war. The philosophical burden that the work is made to carry is probably a result of many additions to the narrative in the form of long discussions and expositions; and it is not unlikely that the idea of a *kala-purusha* as the primary narrator, the depiction of the *kala-chakra* as the central thread of the epic, and the wheel motif have come to be seen as being the very essence of the ancient Indian epic. It appears once again in a powerful and evocative visual form in the ancient sculpture at Sarnath. The *dhamma-chakra* brings the *chakra* of the *kala-purusha* to meet the philosophical reflections of the Buddha. It is interesting to note that the concept of *chakra* pre-dates both the Mahabharata and the Buddha.

The term *chakra* has been traced to the language or languages considered to have been the ancestors of both Sanskrit and Pali. Also several other languages that are believed to have arisen out of the proto-Indo-European—an ancestor of many of the major languages of the world one describes as the 'ancient world'—the languages such as Latin, Greek, Sanskrit, Persian, and several others. Historical Linguistics tell us that 'there was probably a word *kwekwlos*, meaning 'wheel', which is the ancestor of *kuklos* in classical Greek, of *kak*ra in Old Indic and—because 'k' shifts to 'h' in Germanic languages—of *hweohl* in Old English, itself the ancestor of 'wheel' in modern English'. Thus, wheel or *chakra* has been in use in philosophy for those who spoke the earliest form of Greek, Indic and Germanic languages, a concept older than these languages and inherited from an earlier time, an earlier culture, and an earlier language.

It would be, of course, simplistic to imagine that this earlier language or culture was a homogenous one and spread over a vast part of the earth. It would be more appropriate in this respect to imagine that the idea of *chakra* or wheel was of use to many cultures and languages in the period prior to the times we now know as 'ancient times'. Indeed, it was so ever since the rise of agriculture as a dominant mode of production started playing a key role in economies in different parts of what are now known as Europe and Asia. Various researches in archaeology, linguistics, genetics, and related sciences indicate that this period prior to the known ancient times extends between 9,000 years to 6,500 years before our times. Those two or three millennia witnessed the rise of agriculture as a mode of production, and the rise of the concept of *chakra* or wheel. Researches in archaeology and linguistics indicate that it was during these very millennia that humans started developing communication systems based on complex verbal signs.

As to the question of whether human societies had no comparable communication systems prior to this prolonged phase, the answer so far accepted as the most dependable one is that, while there were languages prior to the shift from hunting–gathering economies to pastoral–agrarian economies, practically all of those languages diminished and they were replaced by the pre-ancient languages. These were, as symbolic systems of meaning, not too dissimilar to the languages in use in our time, and were significantly different from the languages before them. Since agriculture was the moving force in the emergence of these languages, let us refer to them, in a purely metaphoric manner, as the *chakra* languages.

THE FEAR OF A SHADOW

The languages of the *chakra* millennia were, as systems of meaning, fairly close to the languages in use in our time. But, we need to enter one caveat here. None of those were ever represented in the form of writing. On the other hand, in our time we have firmly accepted the idea that a mature language is the one that has a well-set system of its representation in writing and therefore capable of getting printed for long-distance distribution. Writing brings natural languages to a new phase of communication. In this form, and particularly when writing is aided by the printing technologies, what is spoken can be carried from one epoch to another, and from one geographical location to another, with a great degree of accuracy. Of course, meanings of words shift from location to location and more decidedly from one epoch to another, but that slide or shift is a limitation—one may even say a gift—that natural languages inherently possess as a kind of birthmark. The very nature of what meaning is makes it impossible to reproduce it in its entirely original form. However, if we set aside this more philosophical difficulty, it becomes clear that writing and all its variations place natural languages into a historical phase that is significantly different from the *chakra* phase. Using, once again, a metaphor, let us call this phase the 'scale' phase, for the emergence of writing is very closely associated with the rise of economic transactions that associated value to production, initially the agricultural production.

Scripts were conceptualized initially to record complicated economic transactions involving production that was beginning to be seen not just as materials but as materials with economic value. It included human labour. It also included inheritance or property. Thus, in ancient times natural languages began to be scripted when the speech communities using them developed production practices giving rise to the concept of 'surplus', 'exchange', and 'value'—all economic values. In ancient Indian mythology, in the Puranic lore as well as in the Buddhist Jatakas, the mention of the merchant class is common. The earliest holders of letters were traders, though subsequently, the writing-classes assumed the functions of legislators and priests. The economic history of the societies in various parts of the world, together with the history of languages that were strengthened by writing as a means to represent speech, has profoundly affected the fate of the natural languages inherited by humans from the pre-ancient times.

The number of natural languages that have come to our time is phenomenally large. It is believed that there are about 6,000 living languages in our time. Not all of them have grammars that fit into a single descriptive framework. Some of these can be described using a grammatical description that we recognize as grammar, while there are such languages that show exceptional behaviour, and if all these exceptions are put together they render a shared grammatical description meaningless. What is common to all those languages, except the sign languages, is that all of them use voice or sound to signify meaning. It is true that writing, which is not speech but only a representation of speech or rather an illusion of sound, removes language from its verbal basis. Yet, without the verbal basis the representation cannot acquire sense. However, various modes of representation of language have impacted 'language as speech'; so much so, that the possibilities of languages that are almost entirely dissociated from speech have started beckoning the human mind. The digital world provides one such possibility.

The digitized exchange of meaning, liberated from sound, can be compared with a shadow play, where shadows signify substance in absence of what the shadows stand for within the visual field of the viewer. The idea that shadow has a remarkable referential capacity and versatile signification ability is not a recent idea. It occurs in Ancient Greek philosophy as it does in the Upanishads. In our time, as the 6,000 living languages are caught in a survival crisis, there is an amazing growth in the universe of the 'shadow-meaning', in the exchange of human thought and memory through a phenomenally speedy exchange of digits. Perhaps, it is an indication of the emergence of an altogether new manner of communication systems.

SCRIPT TRANSGRESSION

Two remarkable recent studies, appearing from somewhat aligned fields, will help us think about what I have tentatively named 'translation time'. One of these is a study of dyslexic children in their early school years by Maryanne Wolf, a professor of Child Development at the Centre for Reading, Tufts University. The study appeared under the title *Proust and the Squid* (2007). The subtitle of Wolf's book is *The Story and Science of the Reading Brain*. After examining the neurological history of reading, she comes to the conclusion that probably the 'non-reading' types are a necessary part of the human evolution. The dyslexics perform, in her opinion, the function of providing the necessary diversity for furtherance of the evolutionary processes. Their relative increase in schooling that focuses on reading skills as the heart of education indicates that after artificial memory started occupying a greater space in man's language transactions, the human brain has started relating to language differently than before. The second study, published a few years later by Michael C. Corballis, is titled *The Recursive Mind: The Origins of Human Language, Thought, and Civilization* (2011). It presents, like Wolf's work, an impressive historical overview of the neurological language ability. Corballis concludes that the recursive character of the human brain has brought it close to a point of fatigue for sound-based language.

These studies point one's attention to the imminent possibility of the human transition from the established manner of language transaction to a new arrangement in the relation between the verbal signs-based language and its interpretations within the human mind/brain. In that new relation, the simultaneity of tenses will become increasingly necessary and expected by the neurological refiguration of cognition, moving communication largely from the language-processing lobe of the brain to image-processing pre-frontal parts of the brain. Faster communication response and sharper abstraction will dominate the process. In simpler words, the human brain is likely to behave more like an intelligent camera, rather than an intelligent teleprinter. These are possibilities that linguists, psychologists, and neurologists are predicting for us. To use once again the simplistic comparison I cited, the camera has much less use for 'before' and 'after' than a teleprinter has.

If indeed, the history of language and the evolution of the human brain point to these possibilities, we are not very far from the time when the idea of a chronological original and its subsequent translation may easily start looking somewhat limited. Within the emerging possibilities of the linguistic shift, it will become necessary to assess and define the phenomenal reality—of space, time and objects—in terms of a non-temporal 'translation time'. In that time, neither script nor speech comes first, nor is either of them subsequent. It will be an interesting time when all originals will be simultaneous with their translations, all translations already embedded within their originals. Bharatamuni of the *Natyashastra* had said that 'the seed of rasa is embedded in the *bhava*', that is, the seed of all that we perceive as knowledge is embedded in the outward representation, the *anukarana,* his idea of translation. All the rest is merely changing the script.

ENDANGERED LANGUAGES
It is a daunting task to determine as to which languages have come closest to the condition of aphasia, which ones are decidedly moving in that direction, and which ones are merely going through the natural linguistic process of transmigration. It may not be inappropriate to say that the

linguistic data available to us is not fully adequate for the purpose. In India, Sir George Grierson's Linguistic Survey of India (1903–1923), material for which was collected in the last decade of the nineteenth century, had identified 179 languages and 544 dialects. The 1921 census reports showed 188 languages and 49 dialects. The 1961 census reports mentioned a total of 1,652 'mother tongues', out of which 184 'mother tongues' had more than 10,000 speakers, and of which 400 'mother tongues' had not been mentioned in Grierson's Survey, while 527 were listed as 'unclassified'. In addition, 103 'mother tongues' were listed as 'foreign'. Earlier, in the 1951 census, the 'foreign' languages found spoken in India were listed at sixty-three, thus showing a 'discovery' of fifty new 'foreign' languages in a matter of a decade. In 1971, the linguistic data offered in the census was distributed in two categories: the officially listed languages of the Eighth Schedule of the Constitution, and the other languages with a minimum of 10,000 speakers each. All other languages, spoken by less than 10,000 speakers, were lumped together in a single entry, 'Others'. That practice continued to be followed in subsequent enumerations. Linguist Uday Narayan Singh comments:

> The problem with Indian labels is that the 1961 Census had floated so many mother tongue labels especially among the unclassified languages that it will have to be worked out as to how many of them finally survived—which is itself a gigantic task. The ones that are spoken above 1,000 speakers have a better chance of survival through later decades, and they included

the following ten unclassified languages: Adibhasha (4,807), Bakerwali (5,941), Beldari (2,702), Jatapu (19,467), Kanjari (1,810), Raj (1,342), Sarodi (1,354), Sohali (1,576), Subba (1,257), and Tirguli (1,000). A few others like Bare (909), Kolhati (952), Khasal (778), Inkari (732), and Uchai (768) are also in a better state. But there were forty-seven others that were not in the same category. There is no doubt that some preliminary verification was done by the census authorities before releasing these names. But still, we may probably have to leave out the 263 language labels that have been returned by less than five speakers. For obvious reasons of their genuineness or difficulty in verification, there will be too many to handle (Singh, 2006).

Language-loss is experienced in India not just by the minor ones and unclassified dialects, but also by major languages that have long literary traditions and a rich heritage of imaginative and philosophical writings. In speech communities that claim major literary languages such as Marathi, Gujarati, Kannada, and Odia as their mother tongues, the younger generations have little or no contact with the written heritage of those languages, while they are able to speak the languages as native speakers.

Language is not only a social system of verbal icons, arbitrarily assembled through ages, it is also a 'means' of carrying forward the cumulative human experience of millennia to the future generations. When language trajectories are snapped, the accumulated wisdom in those languages too gets submerged and continues to survive in severely truncated, irreparable, and insensible forms. Engaged and thought-provoking discussions are taking place in various quarters on the relationship between technology and language, on technology and knowledge, and the emerging forms of knowledge in relation to the future of our planet. If we pay heed to those debates as much more than a mere wish statement, the continuation of some of the potentially threatened languages can be ensured. That shall also contribute significantly to the deepening of democracy in a people-friendly and ecology-friendly form. In human history, language was created as a surplus of man's cognitive and emotive transactions, a product of the labour of the mind. For a significant duration spanning human history, language continued to retain its character as a predominantly free system that is sturdily resistant to government controls, market regulations, and cultural oppressions.

However, over the last few centuries, particularly since the rise of technologies that apparently function as assistance to language transport—printing, photography, electronic-language-storage-and-reproduction, digital-encoding-and-decoding of human language—language-acquisition, language-transmission and language-use have started getting rapidly monetized. Today, as never before, the economically dispossessed classes all over the world are finding it difficult to access language-acquisition as per their needs and desires. Thus, throughout the world, we now notice a digit-powered linguistic class and another print- and digit-deprived linguistic class. The divide is too deep to bridge by following any conventional or prevailing economic ideologies. A technological reversal in the evolution of languages too is a hugely unrealistic proposition. The only hope for ensuring any future for 'linguistic *Homo sapiens*' is to envision together and integrate economic development and linguistic federalism. If the rural landscapes and marginalized communities can be safeguarded, the currently threatened languages will find a safe passage to the future; and only if those languages continue to survive shall we have access to the knowledge that helps us build a sustainable future society—the two are so intimately interlocked.

LANGUAGE DIVERSITY IN DIGITAL FUTURES

India has traditionally been a multilingual area. Neither the Sanskrit language in ancient India nor the Persian language during the seventeenth century were able to displace the large variety of languages that Indians had been using for communication and imaginative expression. During colonial times, the English language entirely replaced the native languages of North America and Australia, but despite such efforts, it did not displace Indian languages. On the contrary, the contact with Sanskrit strengthened Prakrits, the contact with Arabic and Persian brought a rich vocabulary bounty to Indian languages, and the presence and influence of English resulted in an unprecedented efflorescence of literature in the Indian languages. The open spaces and the balanced perspective in the Constitution on the language issue is a testimony to the deep understanding of the cultural and social history of India.

Probably, just as the Industrial Revolution and the associated rise of capitalism in European countries placed the traditional agrarian society at risk, giving rise to the long-drawn conflicts between labour and capital, this great transition facing us globally will create strife, and consequently, violence of an unprecedented order. This time too, the post-human societies are likely to get divided between those with access to the digital and those without it. Already, some linguistic laboratories have started publishing lists of 'digitally dead languages'. Already, the communities not networked are being described as 'non-civil'. The political economies of the world seem to have already resolved that citizens without unique digital identities can be written off as the 'nowhere people'.

It would be tragic if we forgot to look at the struggles and the plight of those who are on the digital fringe. For a very long part of human history, language had continued to retain its character as a predominantly 'free' system that was sturdily resistant to government controls, market regulations, and cultural oppressions.

THE DISCONNECT BETWEEN THE WESTERN AND THE TRADITIONAL

In attempting any comparative study of the Western and Indian knowledge paradigms, a great difficulty one faces is that meanings of the concepts basic to such a discussion are not exactly identical in the two traditions. The terms like 'gnosis', 'logos' and 'philosophy' used in the West are translated in many Indian languages by using terms like *gnan*, *vidya* and *darshan*. 'Philosophy', for instance, refers to a perspective for approaching a set of questions and a logical framework used for understanding a given phenomenon (such as Existence, Universe, Knowledge, Reason, etc.), but *darshan* is closer to vision or the process of viewing rather than the view itself. The difficulty is further compounded by the continuous shift every few centuries, on both sides of the comparison, in the semantic associations constituting these terms. For instance, 'Veda', initially meaning 'knowledge', started indicating 'articulation of knowledge' towards the end of the Vedic period. Given these two formidable difficulties in the field, a comparative view has to rest content with achieving the limited objective of providing overviews rather than offering any great insightful interpretation of the mutual correspondence.

Ever since the modern West came in contact with India, the scholars in this area have been copious and have produced a vast amount of literature on the Indian culture and traditions. Even a cursory survey of all of it would require several volumes. Since making such a survey is not the purpose of the present essay, I shall not venture into commenting on the available corpus of such work. However, as a point of take-off, I allude to Frederic Max Müller's *The Sacred Books of the East* (1879–1910). He was quite generous in complimenting the wisdom found in ancient Indian literature (Müller, 1882). However, the superlative adulation of the India of his imagination was not commonly shared in scholarly circles and he was an exception among his European contemporaries and peers.

The overwhelming majority of European administrators, scholars and researchers of his time had internalized the idea that the British rule was necessary for 'civilizing India', a divine duty fallen upon them which they had accepted as a moral burden. These views, whether negative or superlative, inevitably influenced the self-image of Indian thinkers of the time. Similarly, there was great excitement and acceptance of 'English education' throughout the nineteenth century; on the other hand, a dismissal of Indian forms of knowledge was common among the native literary class in India. The rapidity with which European learning was introduced in Indian colleges and universities through the second half of the nineteenth century led Mahatma Gandhi, during the 1930s, to take a rather uncharacteristic reductive stand in relation to the condition of education in India.

A century later, if one has to take a relatively more objective view of the colonial impact on India's knowledge traditions, two significant elements deserve mention. The first of these is that the pervasive cultural amnesia about India's intellectual failures and accomplishments seems to have hampered the Indian scholar's ability to establish any organic links between the past and the present. For the last two centuries, Indians have either entirely dismissed all that it had cultivated as knowledge in theory, as well as a million everyday tasks. Or there is a tendency to idealize ancient India as possessing comprehensive knowledge across all fields, perpetuating the glorification of an imagined past. The second element is the frequently noticed 'time lag' between the knowledge in the West and that in India and the absence of parity between the knowledge production in the global West and the global South. There are several other countries such as Ireland, Canada, and Australia, which too had to fight the Western attitude of disapproval of the knowledge coming from the former colonies. But the intensity with which Indian scholars have felt it has generally been more acute. However, though the colonial experience can be justifiably held responsible for India's disproportionately low contribution to knowledge during the last two centuries, focusing on colonialism alone may not perhaps yield the complete story of our failure.

For completing the story, one must turn to the text of a lecture that B. R. Ambedkar—a formidable scholar, mass leader and the architect of free India's Constitution—was to (but could not) deliver at Lahore and which was published in the form of a book under the title *Annihilation of Caste* (1936). Ambedkar presents in this work a scathing analysis of social inequalities prevailing in India for over two millennia and a passionate plea for a genuine equality. Dr Ambedkar was probably the most educated of the Indian leaders of his time, with degrees from Columbia and the London School of Economics. To educate the deprived classes for creating an equitable society was one of his non-negotiable articles of faith. Ambedkar's analysis opens up the knowledge question in India, taking it beyond the easily available proof of culpability of the colonial domination, and takes it right to the ancient times when various theological schools inscribed discrimination as a social norm in India. There is no doubt that the caste discrimination in the past, and in the present, and the colonial cultural domination and the continued knowledge imperialism of the West, both had a role in reducing knowledge in India to pauperization, and education in India to a savage mockery of the idea of education.

WHAT IS KNOWLEDGE?

At this stage, I would like to take up the question of what is knowledge as understood in some of the Indian philosophical schools. In the language of philosophy, it is one of those eternally contestable concepts. Its meaning appears to have changed from century to century and from civilization to civilization. What the ancient Babylon and Sumerian people considered knowledge was by no means even half-acceptable to their Greek and Roman successors. If the Greeks based all their sciences on the firm belief that the universe is cubicle in shape, the Europeans after Kepler and Copernicus based theirs on a completely different belief that it is cyclical. In our time, knowledge has more or less entirely rejected those axioms and ideas arising out of them. The term used for describing any profoundly fundamental shift in the very basis of a given body of knowledge is 'epistemic shift'. Despite these periodic epistemic shifts affecting what constitutes knowledge, there has been a relatively steadier idea of knowing. That is to say, knowledge as a verb (which grammatically it is not) is far more constant in its connotation than knowledge as a noun. In this essay, I shall be using knowledge in its verbal sense.

The pre-colonial philosophical thought in India—beginning with the Upanishads and passing through the metaphysical and non-theological *darshan* (schools), Buddhist, Jaina, Sufi world-views, *Bhakti* literature and folk traditions—is replete with the interpretation of what knowing involves. The Bhagavad Gita devotes three chapters, the seventh, eighth and the ninth, to an engaged discussion on what enables us 'to know', what effects knowing has on the knower's consciousness, and how that 'affective knowing' dissolves all dualities leading to a unity between the known and the knower, thus making any 'affective knowing' entirely redundant. *Jnani nityayukta eka bhakti-vishishyate*: 'The man of Knowledge, endowed with constant steadfastness and a single-pointed devotion excels' (Gita, 7.16). The later part of this verse postulates that the Consciousness of the 'trying-to-know' knower and that of the 'all-knowing' knower merge together. Knowledge or *jnana*, therefore, is the dissolution of dualities and attainment of unity.

The *Kena Upanishad* comments on the need for the dissolution of the consciousness 'trying-to-know': *kenesitam patati presitam manah kena pranah prathamah pratiti yuktah*... (Kena, 1.1): 'By who willed and directed does the mind light on its objects? By who commanded does life first move?' In answer to this question, it proposes, 'That which is not thought by the mind but by which, they say, the mind is thought...That which is not seen by the eye but by which the eyes are seen...That which is not heard by the ear but by which the ears are heard...that which is not breathed by life, but by which life breathes; that verily, know thou, is Brahman...' (Radhakrishnan, 1953). Therefore, knowing the Brahman is made the ultimate purpose of knowing of any kind, and knowing anything outside of Brahman is seen as a false knowing or non-knowing. And in the Brahman, there is no individual 'I' but only the pure Cosmic Self, and knowledge can only be subjective and never objective. The *Kena Upanishad* further asserts the perspective by posing a paradox, 'To whomever it is not known, to him it is known; to whomsoever it is known, he does not know,' which, according to S. Radhakrishnan, implies, 'Brahman cannot be comprehended as an object of knowledge. It can be realized as the subject of all knowledge' (Radhakrishnan, 1953). And this is precisely where the Buddha decided to take up an argument with the philosophy of the Upanishads.

When he was the young prince Gautama, Buddha had felt deeply moved by old age, disease, death, and poverty. He left his palace in search of a way of getting beyond these afflictions. He attended sermons in the schools preaching the Upanishadic philosophy, but he remained unsatisfied with the idea of salvation for oneself alone. He continued to wander, sad at heart that he had not found the way as yet. Being struck by a limitless remorse, he decided to fast and meditate on the human condition. The Enlightenment realized by him formed Buddha's 'theory of knowledge'. His state is described in the Buddhist texts as *vajra*-like Samadhi—indestructible concentration—involving a movement from *prajna* (intense intellect), through *karuna* (utmost compassion), to *jnana* (the highest wisdom). The term *jnana* cannot be equated with knowledge. For the Buddha, treading the path from *prajna* to *jnana* is knowledge, both *prajna* and *jnana* by themselves being quite distinct from it. While Buddha did not accept the totality of the Upanishadic Brahman denying the human agency, he did nonetheless accept the idea of knowledge as a process rather than an end-product. Nearly a millennium and a half after Buddha, another remarkable thinker, Abhinavagupta, postulated that 'the knowledge of Truth is just another name for the knowledge of the Self' (Devy, 2002). For him, all experience and all dramatic sentiments were justified in their ability to evoke the experience of that which is of permanent nature, the *sthayibhava* of *moksha*. Knowledge for him was, thus, 'realizing' and not a (or the) 'realization'.

INDIAN KNOWLEDGE PRODUCTION IN THE PAST
Given this emphasis on the process of 'knowing' as the primary justification for the search, whether for Truth or for Self, it was but natural that the pedagogies for inter-generational transmission of wisdom—what we call 'education' and the typologies of what was known or worth knowing—what we call 'disciplines'—were oriented towards quickening the process of knowing rather than consolidating the object called knowledge. Formulation of taxonomies, classification of accumulated knowledge and descriptions of disciplines remain critically dependent on a civilization's understanding of memory. It would, of course, be an injustice to the genius of the ancient Indian scholarship if we overlook the scholars' ability to formulate elaborate schema for every field of knowledge known to them. For instance, the aesthetic experience in drama was classified by Bharata into eight types, the *rasas*, together with the

details of the constant emotions, transitory emotions, and the related actions on stage. In Dhananjaya's *Natyadarsa*, composed several centuries later, there is a further sub-classification of the types of plots, types of heroes, types of actions and so on. In Anandavardhana's *Dhvanyaloka*, we get to see elaborate taxonomies of emotive states, and he expounds in detail the subclasses of 'poetic texture' produced differently by compounds, medium-sized compounds and long compounds. Similarly, the ancient Tamil theoretical text *Tolkappiyam*, of the same period as the *Natyashastra*, has an amazing range of microscopic sub-classification of every aspect of linguistic expression. For instance, it distributes diction into four types as follows:

> Words used in poetry are *Iyarcol*, *Thirisol*, *Thisaiccol*, and *Vadasol*. Of them, *Iyarcol* words are those which are used in conformity with the usage of Tamil and without change in their meanings. The *Thirisol* words are of two kinds which are synonyms and homonyms. *Thisaiccol* or the dialectical words are those which are spoken with their meanings unchanged in the twelve divisions of Tamil land where correct Tamil is in use. The words of Northern languages, *Vadasol*, become fit to be used in Tamil when they adopt the Tamil phonetics discarding their northern ones (Devy, 2003).

One could not have asked for more elaborate taxonomy of dialects and their literary use. This kind of minute classification marks all fields of knowledge in the ancient and medieval India including medicine, physiology, botany, chemistry, metallurgy, linguistics, mathematics, astronomy, drama, dance and music. The fields of knowledge went through a number of modifications during the medieval times, particularly after the main languages of knowledge transactions—Tamil, Pali, Sanskrit—were replaced by the modern Indian languages such as the modern Tamil, Malayalam, Telugu, Kannada, Marathi, Gujarati, Bangla, Odia, Assamiya, Punjabi, Kashmiri, etc. New categories were added to the previously existing taxonomies and some of the earlier categories were dropped. This transition is most evident from the eleventh to the thirteenth century. Thus, Abhinavagupta added the *shant-rasa* as an aesthetic experience to the gamut proposed by Bharata a millennium before him; Mammata added more subtypes to Dhananjaya's classification of poetic arts; the poet-saints added further concepts to the previously existing range of metaphysical concepts; musicians added more *ragas*, *gatis*—musical structures and patterns; the cartographers added new ways of doing cartography; arithmetic accepted a range of new weights, measures, and units of counting.

This process of renewing and expanding the established disciplines was significantly quickened particularly after paper came into use as a means for recording computations, archives, circulating philosophical arguments and writing treatises. This is exactly how knowledge deepens in a given civilization and disciplines of knowledge evolve. It should be mentioned, however, that the schools of thought taken into account in the foregoing discussion have all been based on certain iconic texts available to us. It is these iconic texts that form in part the basis of the history of Indian philosophy, literature, and culture. The history has remained seriously lopsided as it does not take into account the knowledge traditions of the communities that were left out of the spectrum of formal education and knowledge production. Here, the term 'formal education' is not being used to mean 'institutional education.' It is also not being used in order to draw a distinction between the oral traditions and the written traditions of knowledge. In India, the majority of significant texts were transmitted through oral recitations until printing became a widely adopted method of reproducing texts. Hence, in the pre-modern Indian context, the term 'formal' should be understood as having a significantly different connotation. It points to the distinction between 'oral, but sanctified or canonized' and 'oral, but non-canonized'.

The non-canonized knowledge traditions belonged to the larger sections of the knowledge-producers, mainly the indigenous communities—the Adivasis—and the communities that were stigmatized as untouchables—the Shudras. These communities, as they uneasily coexisted with the non-Shudras—continued to develop their own technique of dealing with the natural forces and the natural resources. They developed their own stories of origin of the world and their independent cosmologies, leading to their own interpretation of the universe and the concepts like 'time' and 'space'. Though the Vedas had in them seventy-two metrical forms of verse, the non-canonized communities developed their own meters. Though Bharata had provided the theoretical framework for theatre performance through his *Natyashastra*, the non-canonized continued to develop their entirely different forms of theatre. Though the Ayurveda had evolved a certain kind of understanding of the human body, the non-canonized evolved their own, and strikingly different, understanding of the human anatomy. All of such knowledge was brought forward through generations of the non-canonized, through apprenticeship and oral transmission. But in these communities, the attitude to the distinction between knowledge and labour was remarkably different from the one that prevailed among the holders of the canonized knowledge. As a result, a single and comprehensive formulation of an Indian body of universal knowledge remained unattainable in the pre-modern India.

Yet, it is possible to argue that though the sanctified memory and the non-sanctified memory continued to exist and grow in largely unrelated cannons, the creation of any universal knowledge was not the primary objective of the pursuit of knowledge in India. This counter-argument, entirely valid as it is, would point to the centrality given to intuition in acquiring knowledge. The knowledge traditions, in all cannons, whether tribal, agrarian, shamanic, Buddhist, Nyaya, Jaina, Sankhya or Upanishadic, all maintained that the fountainhead of knowledge is the individual consciousness. It springs from within, for it is *apriori* to the human consciousness, already in the being. The Bhagavad Gita states unambiguously that 'knowledge is to be seen getting realized, which the confused ones never do. It is only those who approach it with their *gnana-chakshu* can see it.' *Utkramantam sthitam vapi bhunjanam va gunanvitam. Vimudha-nanu pashyanti, pashyati gnanachakshu-sah* (Adhyaya-15, verse-10). It does not dawn upon but emerges or springs up, as the *sphota* theory of meaning most eloquently proposes. Hence, various knowledge traditions spoke of the *gnan-chakshu* (the knowledge-eye which opens through concentration). In this process, intuition and not memory acquires primacy. There was one exception though to India's adherence to intuition as the non-negotiable foundation of knowledge. It emerged from the Lokayata School of the materialists initiated by Charvaka. Describing the intellectual ethos of India during the closing centuries of the millennium before Christ, Wendy Doniger states:

> A number of groups engaged in friendly intellectual combat at this time. Those were probably early adherents of what were to become the six major philosophical schools of Hinduism: Critical Inquiry (Mimansa), Logic (Nyaya), Particularism (Vesisika), Numbers (Sankhya), Yoga and Vedanta. Ajivikas (contemporaries of Jainas and Buddhists) rejected free will, an essential component of the doctrine of Karma. Lokayatas (This 'worldly' people also called Materialists and Charvakas, followers of the founder named Charvaka) not only rejected the doctrine of reincarnation...but believed that physical sense data were the only source of knowledge.... (Doniger, 2009).

However, in the subsequent centuries, the followers of the Lokayatas were driven out of the social fold and the intellectual debates. The memory based universal knowledge, an objective stock of which civilizations seek to build, has correspondingly objective ways of validation. But, validation of intuition through no objective criteria is possible. Therefore, the measure of authenticity, the mark of validation and the ways of recognizing new theory in Indian traditions of knowledge depended primarily on approval by the peers or superiors in the intuition networks. And, almost invariably, the knower in India vouched fulfilment by claiming that what he knew as new knowledge had all been there in tradition, known already by his forerunners. India's exposure to the Western forms of knowledge during the colonial era and the confrontation between the two distinct traditions of knowledge within the framework of the unequal relationship brought the validity of Indian knowledge cannons close to a crisis of existence. Acknowledging it, Jawaharlal Nehru records in his *Discovery of India,* that while the British rulers had been far less civilized in the past as compared to the precolonial Indians, during the two centuries of the colonial era a new phenomenon had been arising in Europe and energizing the British. It was the phenomenon called 'modernity':

> There was more literacy in India than in England or the rest of Europe, though education was strictly traditional. Probably, there were more civic amenities also. The general condition of the masses in Europe was very backward and deplorable and compared unfavourably with the conditions prevailing in India. But there was this vital difference: new forces and living currents were working invisibly in Western Europe,

bringing change in their train; in India, conditions were far more static (Nehru, 1946).

Once begun towards the close of the eighteenth century, the vital difference continues to remain unabridged to our time.

NOTES

1. In 1961 when the census was carried out, India reported the existence of 1,652 mother tongues. In 1971 the census (decadal census) reported only 109 mother tongues. How did the census statistics come down from 1,652 to 109? Is it because of the fact that the government had failed in this instance? The census reports are usually published five or six years after the census is recorded. So the 1971 census was published either in 1976 or in 1977. In 1971 a war had taken place outside India which resulted in the splitting up of East Pakistan and West Pakistan. East Pakistan became a separate nation on the question of language. Bangla was not allowed in the education in East Pakistan and therefore East Bengal became Bangladesh. Since this had happened next door the Government of India became very apprehensive about the language diversity. So when the 1971 census data was published, it disclosed statistics for only those languages spoken by more than ten thousand. Thus it reported only 108 languages; 109th was described as 'all others', which included the remaining thousand languages and more. Children, who are born into these other languages, will, therefore, never get schooling in their own mother tongues. It is obligatory on the part of the Government of India to provide money only for education on languages listed in the Eighth Schedule of the Constitution. So there are no schools, colleges and universities for other languages though occasionally there are radio programmes in other languages. Children do not learn their own mother tongues and instead learn some other languages. They are hesitant to disclose other languages as their mother tongue. Languages are dying in this fashion. We have as of today about 700 languages in this country. As per the forecast of 'Ethnologue' (a renowned website) and of UNESCO, by the end of this century, India will have possibly not more than one tenth of the languages left; think of about 800 dying languages!

What do these languages hold in them? They hold knowledge about ecology. I was compiling a list of Himalayan languages in three states—Jammu and Kashmir, Himachal Pradesh, and Uttarakhand—and found that there are numerous terms for snow. They have a word for snow which falls on muddy waters, snow which falls in the latter part of the afternoon, the first and last phase of snow and so on. All these indicate great knowledge of ecology in these days when we are all worried about climate change and global warming. We are losing or we are bound to lose such information.

2. Untraced Mother Tongues (1961): Abhahatik, Adnis, Agsula, Ahenai, Aia, Alam, Anharic, Araji, Ascrini, Ashai, Ashia, Aurkhati, Badhri, Baha, Bakatan, Balhapuri, Baliyani, Balvan, Bandubal, Bangargi, Bangarni, Banor, Banthli, Barai, Barochi, Basali, Bask, Basti, Bavari, Bhadruvali, Bhagwati, Bhamti, Bhigoli, Bhivadi, Bhohoe, Bithalanean, Biyogi, Bojwari, Bolti Zaban, Bomba, Bunhar, Canthars, Chabeli, Chachi, Chetori, Chhushmeni, Chotanagpuri, Chovoel, Chow, Ciol, Commanga, Dalue, Damal, Darchini, Dati, Dehati, Deke, Derasmati, Dhallu, Dichi, Dulai, Dunavi Pahari, Dwed Boli, Elonguria, Fatma, Fernada, Fugian, Fulnagri, Gadal, Gagar, Gangasi, Gaunti, Gavari, Ghamoli, Ghanjhari, Ghircharg, Gorhathi, Godhami, Gohari, Gosai, Gusara, Guthara, Hali, Halvado, Hamar, Hanemadi, Hardasi, Hasang, Heirlese, Helgo, Hengna, Hijomdel, Hungyo, Jamthali, Jarasi, Jawali Pahari, Jhalo Malo, Jhora, Jogsani, Jokhri, Jord, Junkuku, Kaisid, Kalazan, Kalwi, Kamadun, Kamat, Kandri, Kanki, Kansale, Kapati, Karai, Karwali, Katwi, Kaw, Kawami, Khampa, Khanali, Kharkhadi, Khattai, Kigoi, Kmer, Kosan, Kristi, Ksarwar, Kudu, Kumadri, Kunali, Kundh, Kunija, Kunsar, Kutal, Lagodu, Lalgi, Langu, Libo, Laosi, Laosia, Logli, Loher, Lunkhul, Madgi, Mahaswali, Mai, Makhiya, Malantha, Malnuti, Malsan Pahari, Maltis, Mandakini, Mani, Mar, Marahi, Mashan, Masti, Matrai, Mehari, Melashi, Metali, Miji, Mikum, Mita, Molu, Momidomi, Mompa, Morma, Moung, Mumhara, Muslim Pahari, Muttari, Myalor, Nagi, Nakkala, Narmadiya, Nasang Ki Boli, Nasuka, Nayakula, Neglo, Neof, Ngaite, Nudiya, Padhakhy, Pahari Tikkari, Parachinari, Pargar, Parui, Pasoba, Patsani Pahari, Pawite, Phaktun, Pokrine, Qustash, Rakchhai, Ramdasi, Ranat, Rebucheba,

Rovabi, Rumai, Sanap, Sanku, Sapru, Sarnarthi, Sasi, Saswari, Savaji, Sayeng, Seema, Sellum, Sengou, Servari, Seypho, Shaja, Sigitvia, Sinos, Somasahag, Sonni, Sujathigar, Sulung, Sungi, Sunkarad, Surali, Swani, Taban, Taharine, Talami, Tandil, Tanjarvalngo, Tankera, Tarane, Taroa, Tashwar, Tayeng, Temelly, Tepali, Thakai, Thari, Thatma, Thatwari, Topi, Trimali, Trivedi, Tungo, Ujra, Umarpala, Urani, Uravan, Usthu, Vadakkali, Vaipaki, Vaival, Varanchiti, Vatu, Wakarali, Walli, Walmiki, Wandgiri, Yahudi, Yaskhila, and Zunwar.

3. The term 'return' in its administrative technical sense means 'register/stat/present', normally used during the census process, official surveys, etc.
4. 'Raw Returns' is the heading that the census uses for 'unprocessed' mother tongue names. After they are processed by the Linguistics cell of the census office, they are called 'Mother Tongues', and after a further and more refined processing, they are called 'languages'.
5. 'When the Constituent Assembly adopted the Constitution of India on 26 November 1949, there were fourteen languages listed in the Eighth Schedule of the Indian Constitution. They were (in the order of number of speakers): Hindi, Telugu, Bengali, Marathi, Tamil, Urdu, Gujarati, Kannada, Malayalam, Odia, Punjabi, Kashmiri, Assamese, and Sanskrit. There have been three amendments to the Eighth Schedule during the last fifty-five years, the results of which have been as follows. Sindhi was included through the Constitution Amendment Bill No 21 in 1967, Konkani, Manipuri and Nepali (or, Gorkhali) through Amendment Bill No. 71 in 1992, and Maithili, Santali, Bodo, and Dogri through Amendment Bill No. 100 in 2003' (Singh 2006b).
6. Indian population stood at 1.21 billion in 2011. ***Censusindia.gov/2011-prov-results/indiaatglance.html*** visited on 25 January 2021.
7. The use of language is predicated in humans on the expression of the FOXP2 and CNTNAP2 genes and the population frequency of two brain growth and development genes, ASPM and Microcephalin, but the array of possibilities for language use is limited only by cognitive complexity. However, fortunately, the human brain at approximately 1,350 cc has evolved just for the management of such complexity, and in the human brain, the temporal lobe is 23 per cent larger than other

brain regions and four times larger than that of our closest mammalian relatives, the chimpanzees. Linguists and cognitive neuroscientists have also determined which regions of the human brain are involved in which parts of speech with some degree of precision. For example, the understanding of proper nouns is thought to occur in the anterior and medial areas of the temporal lobe, and that of common nouns on the lateral and inferior temporal lobes.

8. The Russian linguist N. S. Trubetzkoy developed the concept of 'Language Area'. This English term is not what he used. His conceptual framework was used by Bernard Bloch, Roman Jacobson, Franz Boas, and Edward Sapir. It was applied by M. B. Emeneau in 1953 to explain the mutual influence of various Indian languages in close contact. Explaining his use of the term 'area', he states:

> The use of classifiers can be added to those other linguistic traits previously discussed, which establish India as one linguistic area for historical study. The evidence is at least as clear-cut as any that has been advanced in the establishment of a linguistic area in any part of the world, and in fact a good deal more so than much that has been offered. It is to be hoped that it will not be neglected henceforth when the question is raised whether linguistic features, especially those of morphology and syntax, can diffuse across genetic boundaries. Some of the features presented here are, it seems to me, as 'profound' as we could wish to find (if we must attempt to apply Sapir's value criteria). Certainly, the end result of the borrowings is that the languages of the two families, Indo-Aryan and Dravidian, seem in many respects more akin to one another than Indo-Aryan does to the other Indo-European languages. In another place I adumbrate an attempt to include the linguistic area India in the larger linguistic area of East, Southeast, and South Asia. The evidence so far found concerns the use of classifiers and makes it at least possible that this trait reached the Indo-Aryan languages of the Magadhan area from Southeast Asia; but the demonstration of this is not as clear as that of the relationships

within India and need not be given here to obscure the clear outlines of the matter.

9. Some of the sections of this essay are based on my published book *The Crisis Within: Knowledge and Education in India* (Aleph, 2017), and *After Amnesia* (Orient Blackswan, 1992).

BIBLIOGRAPHY

Abrams, M. H. (1954), *The Mirror and the Lamp.* New York: Oxford University Press.

Ambedkar, B. R. (1970), *Who were the Shudras: How they Came to be the fourth Varna in the Indo-Aryan Society,* p. 242. Bombay: Thackers.

———, (1936), Undelivered Speech prepared by B. R. Ambedkar.

Anthony, David W. (2010), *The Horse, the Wheel, and Language: How Bronze-Age Riders from the Eurasian Steppes Shaped the Modern World.* New Jersey: Princeton University Press.

Asp, Elissa D. and De Villiers, Jessica (2010), *When Language Breaks Down.* New York: Cambridge University Press.

Austin, Granville (2009), 'Language and the Constitution: the half-hearted compromise'. In Asha Sarangi (ed.) *Language & Politics in India,* pp. 41-92. New Delhi: Oxford University Press.

Austin, Peter (2008), *One Thousand Languages: living, endangered and lost.* Berkley: University of California Press.

Austin, Peter K. and Stuart McGill (eds.) (2011), *Endangered Languages.*London: Routledge.

Balkrishnan. R. (2022), *Journey of a Civilisation.* 3rd (edn.) Chennai: Roja Muthiah Research Library, pp. 266-67.

Barber, Charles, Joan C. Beal, and Philip Shaw (1993), *The English Language: a historical introduction.* Cambridge: Cambridge University Press.

Bellwood, Peter (2013), *First Migrants: Ancient Migration in Global*

Perspective. Chichester, U.K: Wiley Blackwell.

Bianco, Joseph Lo (2012), 'National Language Revival Movements: reflections from India, Israel, Indonesia and Ireland'. In Bernard Spolsky (ed.) *The Cambridge Handbook of Language Policy,* pp. 501-522.Cambridge: Cambridge University Press.

Blake, William (1804), reprinted (1808), *Jerusalem: The Emanation of the Giant- 'Then the Divine Hand' showing Christ soaring above Albion within whose bosom 'the Divine hand found the Two Limits, Satan and Adam'*. Self-published.

Blench, Roger and Mathew Spriggs (eds.) (1999–2012), *Archaeology and Language: theoretical and methodological orientations,* 4 vols. Abingdon and New York: Routledge.

Bragg, Melvyn (2003), *The Adventure of English: the biography of a language*. London: Hodder & Stoughton.

Braggs, I. and Freedman,H. I. (1993), 'Can the Speakers of a Dominated Language Survive as Unilinguals? A Mathematical Model of Bilingualism'. In *Mathematical and Computer Modeling* Vol. 18, (6), pp. 9-18. Oxford: Pergamon Press.

Caldwell, Robert (1956), *A Comparative Grammar of the Dravidian or South-Indian Family of Languages*. Madras: University of Madras.

Campbell, Lyle (2019), How Many Language Families are there in the World? In *Anuario del Seminario de Filología Vasca 'Julio de Urquijo',* 52 (1/2) p.133. Spain: UPV/EHU Press.

Censusindia.gov/2011-prov-results/indiaatglance.htmlvisited on 25 January 2021.

Chappell, Tim (ed.) (1996), *The Plato reader*. Edinburgh: Edinburgh University Press.

Chitre, Dilip (tr. &ed.) (1991), *Says Tuka: Selected Poems of Tukaram*. Pune: Sontheimer Cultural association.

Coleridge, Samuel Taylor (1817), *The Biographia Literaria*.

Corballis, Michael C. (2011), *The Recursive Mind: The Origins of Human Language, Thought, and Civilization,* p.126. Princeton: Princeton University Press.

Cru, Josep (ed.) (2010), *The Management of Linguistic Diversity and Peace Processes.* Barcelona: UNESCOCAT.

Crystal, David (2000), *Language Death.* Cambridge: Cambridge University Press.

Dalby, Andrew (2003), *Language in Danger.* New York: Columbia University Press.

Deshpande, C. R. (1978), *Transmission in the Mahabharata tradition: Vyasa and Vyasids.* Simla: Indian Institute of Advanced Studies.

———, Madhav M. (1993), *Sanskrit & Prakrit Sociolinguistic Issues.* Delhi: Motilal Banarsidass Publishers.

Devy, G. N. (1998), *After Amnesia: Tradition and Transformation in Indian Literary Criticism*: Orient Longman, Bombay: 1992.

———, *Of Many Heroes: An Indian Essay in Literary Historiography.* Hyderabad: Orient Longman.

———, (ed.) (2003), *Indian Literary Criticism: Theory and Interpretation.* New Delhi: Orient Longman.

———, Devy, *Indian Literary Criticism*, p.16.

———, (2003), *The Painted Words: An Anthology of Tribal Literature.* USA: Penguin Group.

Devy, *The Painted Words*, p. 16.

———, (2004) "Truth in India", in *Keywords: Truth*, ed. By Nadia Tazi. Newyork: The Other Press.

———, (2009), 'India: Layered Inequalities'. In Volkman, Toby Alice (ed.) *Origins, journeys and returns: social justice in international higher education.* New York: Social Science Research Council.

———, (2009), "The Being of Bhasha", In the *G. N. Devy Reader*. New Delhi: Orient Blackswan.

———, (2014), *The Being of Bhasha: general introduction to the People's Linguistic Survey of India*. New Delhi: Orient Blackswan.

———, (2017), *The Crisis Within: On Knowledge and Education in India*. New Delhi: Aleph.

Devy, G. N. (ed.) (2014-2024), *The People's Linguistic Survey of India*. New Delhi: Orient Blackswan.

Devy, G. N., Davis, Geoffrey V., and Chakravarty K.K. (eds.) *Indigeneity: Culture and Representation*. New Delhi: Orient Black Swan.

Devy, G. N., Tony Joseph and Ravi Korisettar (ed.) (2023), *The Indians: Histories of a Civilization*. New Delhi: Aleph Book Company.

Devy, *The Indians*, pp. 17–18.

Devy, *The Indians*, pp. 68–69.

Devy, *The Indians*, p. 59.

Devy, *The Indians*, p. 240.

Devy, *The Indians*, p. 142.

Devy, *The Indians*, p. 208.

Devy, *The Indians*, pp. 206–7.

Doniger, Wendy (2015), *The Hindus: An Alternative History*, p.185. New Delhi: Speaking Tiger.

Ellis, Francis Whyte (2023), *Dissertation The Second On the Malaylma Language*. Bombay: Legare Street Press.

Emeneau. M. B. (1956), 'India as a Linguistic Area'. In Language, Vol. 32, No.1, pp. 3-16. New York: Linguistic Society of America.

Eisenstadt, S. N., Kahane, R., and Shulam, D., (eds.) (1984), *Orthodoxy, Heterodoxy and Dissent in India*. Berlin and New York: Mouton.

Estrada, Gabriel (2009), 'Classical, Modern and Transnational Nahuatl Literatures'. In Fishman, Joshua A. (ed.) (2001), *Can Threatened Languages be Saved?*.U.K.: Multilingual Matters.

Florey, Margaret (ed.) (2010), *Endangered Languages of Australia.* New York: Oxford University Press.

Gibbon, Edward (1776), *The History of the Decline and Fall of the Roman Empire.* London: Strahan William & Cadell Thomas.

Gillespie, Tarleton (2007), *Wired Shut: copyright and the shape of digital culture.* Cambridge, Massachusetts: The MIT Press.

Gordon, Raymond G. (2005), *Ethnologue: Languages of the World.* Dallas: SIL International.

Harrison, K. David (2007), *When Languages Die.* New York: Oxford University Press.

Hobbes, Thomas (1651), *Leviathan or The Matter, Forme and Power of a Commonwealth Ecclesiasticall and Civil, commonly referred to as Leviathan.* Printed in numerous editions from century to century.

Janse, Mark, and Tol Sijmen (eds.) (2003), *Language Death and Language Maintenance: theoretical practice and descriptive approaches.* Amsterdam/Philadelphia: John Benjamin Publishing Company.

Jones, Sir William (1807), *The Works of Sir William Jones: With the Life of the Author by Lord Teignmouth, Volume 5.* Cambridge: Cambridge Library Collection.

Joseph, Tony (2018), *Early Indians: The Story of Our Early Ancestors and Where We Came From.* New Delhi: Juggernaut.

Kothiyal, Tanuja (2016), *Nomadic Narratives: A History of Mobility and Identity in the Great Indian Desert,* Cambridge: Cambridge University Press.

Lacan, Jaques (1977), *Ecrits: a selection.* Alan Sheridan (tr.). New York: W. W. Norton.

Lukanovic, Sonja Noval (ed.) (2010), *A Shared Vision: international dialogue—a global paradigm to promote linguistic and cultural diversity.* Ljubljana: Institute for Ethnic Studies.

Lyotard, Jean-Francois (1984), *The Postmodern Condition: A Report on Knowledge.* Geoff Bennington and Brian Massumi (trs.). Manchester: Manchester University Press.

Masson, J. L., and M. V. Patwardhan (1969), *Santarasa and Abhinava's philosophy.* Pune: The Oriental Institute.

Max Muller, Frederick (1879-1910), *The Sacred Books of the East.* 50 Vols. p.10. Oxford: Oxford University Press.

Max Muller, Frederick (1882), *India: What Can It Teach Us?* New York: Funk and Wagnalls.

Mayhew, Arthur (1926), *The Education of India: a survey of British education policy in India, 1835-1920, and its bearing on national life and problems in India today.* London: Faber and Gwyer.

McMahon, April, and McMahon Robert (2013), *Evolutionary Linguistics.* Cambridge: Cambridge University Press.

Meierkord, Chritiane (2012), *Interactions across Englishes: Linguistic Choices in Local and International Contact Situations.* New York: Cambridge University Press.

Mosley, Christopher (2010), *The Atlas of the World Languages in Danger.* UNESCO.

Naik, J. P, and Nurullah Syed (1951), *A History of British Education in India during the British Period.* Bombay: Popular.

Nandy, Ashis and Jahanbegloo Ramin (2022), *Talking India: Ashis Nandy in Conversation with Ramin Jahanbegloo.* New Delhi: Oxford University Press.

Nehru, Jawaharlal (1946), *The Discovery of India.* Calcutta: The Signet Press.

Nettle, Daniel and Romaine, Suzanne (2000), *Vanishing Voices.*

Oxford: Oxford University Press.

Nigam, R. C. (1972), 'Language Handbook on Mother Tongues in Census', In *Census of India 1971*, No. 10. New Delhi: Census Centenary Monographs.

Panini, Fourth century BCE. *The Ashtadhyayi of Panini*. Srisha Chandra Vasu (tr.). Reprinted (2018) London: Forgotten Books.

Phipps, Peter (2009), 'Garma and Beyond: Indigenous Cultural Festivals for Decolonization'. In Devy, G.N., Davis, Geoffrey V., and Chakravarty K. K. (eds.) *Indigeneity: Culture and Representation*. New Delhi: Orient Black Swan.

Radhakrishnan, S. (1953),*The Principal Upanishads*, pp. 582–3. Indian edition (1989). Delhi: Oxford University Press.

Radhakrishnan, *The Principal Upanishads*, p. 585.

Ramanujan, A. K. (1992), 'Annayya's Anthropology'. *From Cauvery to Godavary: Modern Kannada Short stories*. Narayan Hegde, (tr.) New Delhi: Penguin Books.

Rathore, Akash Singh and Nandy, Ashis (2018), *Vision for a Nation: Paths and Perspectives*. New Delhi: Penguin.

Regh, Kenneth and Campbell, Lyle (2018), *The Oxford Handbook of Endangered Languages*. Oxford: Oxford University Press.

Rege, Sharmila (2013), *Against the Madness of Manu: B. R. Ambedkar's Writings on Brahminical Patriarchy*. Delhi: Navayana.

Reich, David (2018), *Who We Are and How We Got Here: Ancient DNA and the New Science of the Human Past*. Oxford: Oxford University Press.

Robinson, Andrew (2009), *Lost Languages: The Enigma of The World's Undeciphered Scripts*. London: Thames and Hudson.

Rossi, Paolo (2006), *Logic and the Art of Memory: The Quest for a Universal Language,* p. 192. London: Athlone Press.

Sarangi, Asha (ed.) (2009), *Language and Politics in India*. New

Delhi: Oxford University Press.

Schreier, Daniel et al. (eds.) (2010), *The Lesser Known Varieties of English*, New York: Cambridge University Press.

Schwartzberg, Joseph E. (2009), 'Factors in the Linguistic Reorganization of Indian States'. In Asha Sarangi (ed.) *Language and Politics in India*. New Delhi: Oxford University Press.

Sengupta, Kamalini (ed.) (2010), *Endangered Languages in India*. New Delhi: INTACH.

Singh, Uday Narayan (2006), 'Minor and Minority Languages in India'. Report by G.N. Devy Sub-Group, *Protecting Non-Scheduled Languages*, Eleventh Five Year Plan Proposal. New Delhi: Ministry of Human Resource Development.

———, (2006b), 'Status of Lesser-known Languages in India'. Anju, Saxena and Lars, Borin (eds.) *Lesser-Known Languages of South Asia*. Berlin: De Gruyter Mouton.

Stilz, Gerhard (2009), 'Friends, Indigenes and Others: A German Interjection'. G. N. Devy et al. (eds.) *Indigeneity: Culture and Representation*. New Delhi: Orient Black Swan.

Trubetzkoy, N. S. (1939), 'Gedanken über das Indogermanenproblem'. *Acta Linguistica* (*Hafniensa*) 1.81-9.

Visvanathan, Shiv (2009), 'Listening to the Pterodactyl'. In G. N. Devy et al. (eds.) *Indigeneity: Culture and Representation*. New Delhi: Orient Black Swan.

Wolf, Maryanne (2007), *Proust and the Squid: The Story and Science of the Reading Mind*. New York: Harper Collins.

Wurn, Stephen (2005), *Atlas of the World's Languages in Danger*. Paris: UNESCO.

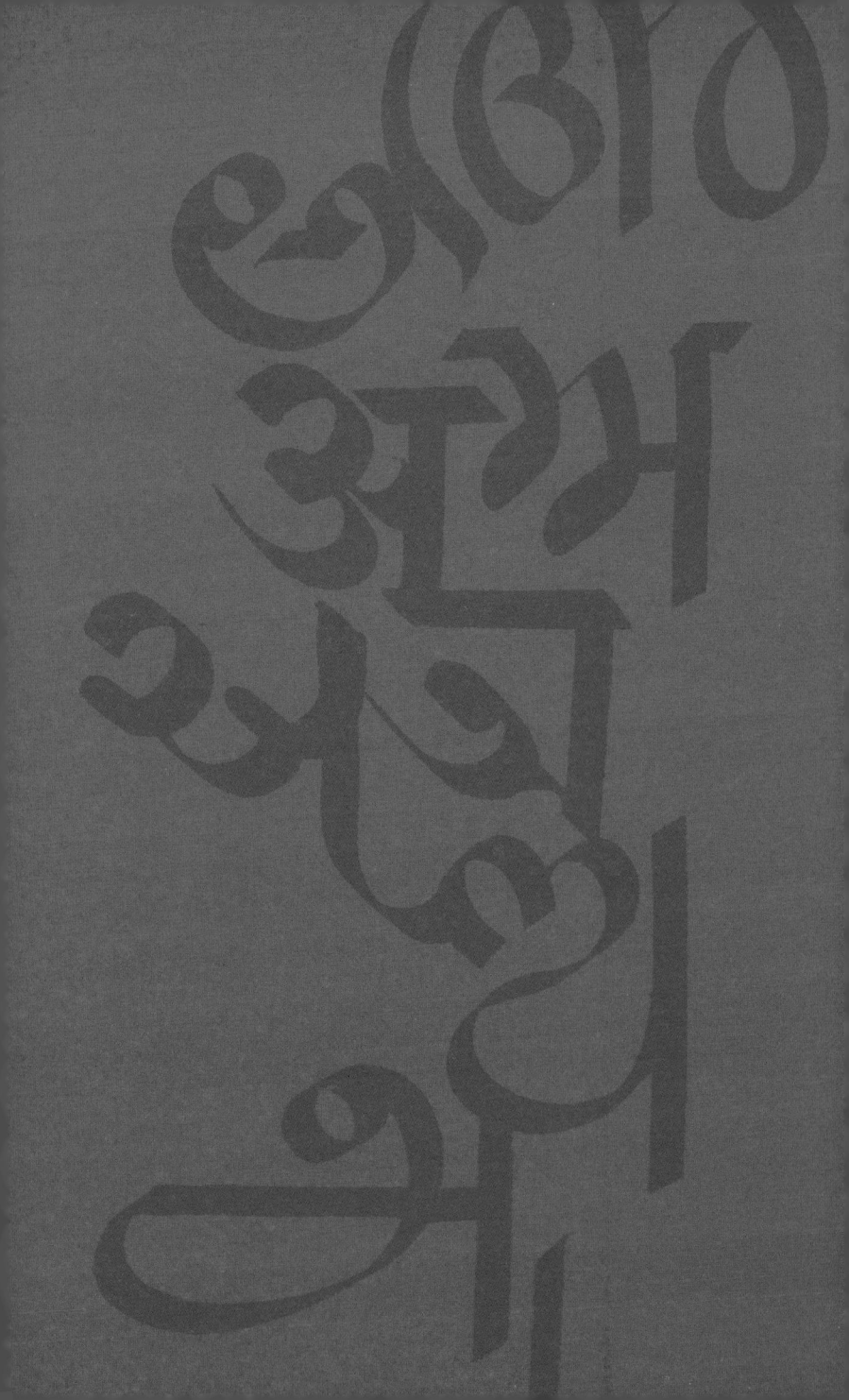